HOME SWEET HOME

HOME SWEET HOME

The Vanessa-Ann Collection

BALLANTINE BOOKS • NEW YORK

Tece —

I wanted to write this dedication for you
but somehow I simply could not find the words,
so I borrowed these from Heidi.

> *You painted me*
> *a childlike picture*
> *of tomorrow*
> *and signed it*
> *with a polished*
> *light blue crayon*
> *so that I might*
> *see,*
> *reach,*
> *believe*
> *and dream.*

I love you.
Jo —

Our special thanks to
Mrs. J. E. Rich
Boyd and Susan Bingham
J. Scott Buehler

Produced for Ballantine Books by THE VANESSA-ANN COLLECTION: Terrece Beesley Woodruff, Owner, Designer • Jo Packham, Owner, Designer • Margaret Shields Marti, Executive Editor, Designer • Monica Smith, Editor • Trice Liljenquist Boerens, Art Director, Designer • Nancy Whitley, Needlework Director, Designer • Julie Truman, Graphic Artist, Designer • Susan Jorgensen, Graphing Director • Pam Randall, Operations Director • Barbara Milburn, Administrative Assistant • Kathi Allred, Customer Relations • Ryne Hazen, Photographer

Library of Congress Catalog Number: 87-91831
ISBN: 0-345-34996-2
Manufactured in the United States of America.
First Edition: October 1988

10 9 8 7 6 5 4

CONTENTS

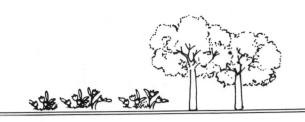

Ask several different people what it takes to make a house a home and you will get several different answers.

"Home to me is a simple, funny little house in upstate Maine."

"Ours is a warehouse loft in Greenwich Village."

"Mine is timeless and beyond style."

"Mine is gently nostalgic."

"We love a rural Texas retreat."

"Ours is serene, dignified and refined."

"We found a once-forgotten barn in Minnesota."

A home, no matter where, and regardless of style, is a house made of a million moments.

A baby's squeal at firelight,

children playing in falling leaves of autumn,

a daughter's first love,

the day your son announced, "I made the team,"

and the laughter of old friends.

A home is the story of the people who live there, recorded for all to remember in letters written to those who have long since gone their way, in photographs gently placed between album pages, and in stitches taken on handspun cotton or antique linen.

...a welcome place to rediscover relationships rich in tradition.

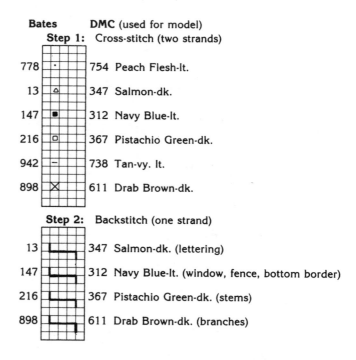

Bates		DMC (used for model)	
		Step 1:	Cross-stitch (two strands)
778	·	754	Peach Flesh-lt.
13	⌂	347	Salmon-dk.
147	▪	312	Navy Blue-lt.
216	▫	367	Pistachio Green-dk.
942	−	738	Tan-vy. lt.
898	✕	611	Drab Brown-dk.
		Step 2:	Backstitch (one strand)
13		347	Salmon-dk. (lettering)
147		312	Navy Blue-lt. (window, fence, bottom border)
216		367	Pistachio Green-dk. (stems)
898		611	Drab Brown-dk. (branches)

MODEL Stitch on cream Aida 14. The finished design size is 5⅛" × 6⅛". Cut the fabric 11" × 13". Finished design sizes for other fabrics are Aida 11—6½" × 7¾"; Aida 18—4" × 4¾"; Hardanger 22—3¼" × 3⅞".

71–Stitch Count

85

MODEL Stitch on driftwood Belfast Linen 32. The finished design size is 12″ × 18½″. Cut the fabric 20″ × 27″. Begin stitching Section I 6″ from the top edge and 4″ from the left edge.

SECTION I

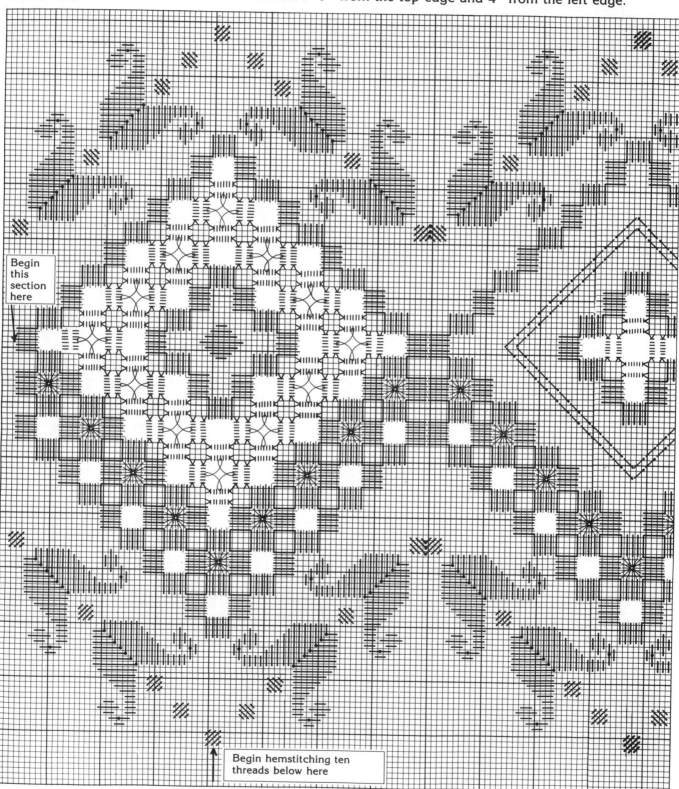

Begin this section here

Begin hemstitching ten threads below here

... a mosaic of simple moments, a love affair with quality...

Center of design

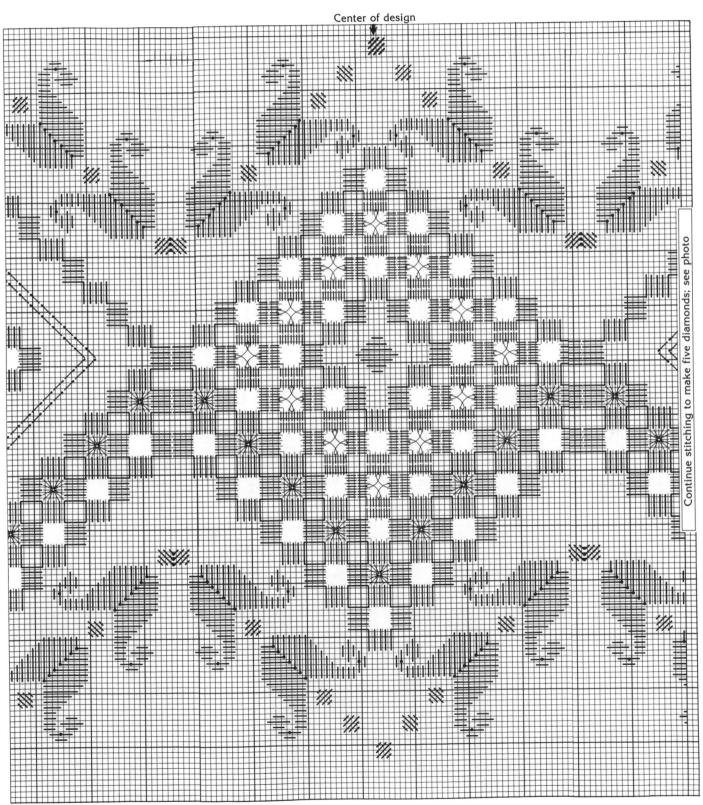

Continue stitching to make five diamonds; see photo

SECTION II

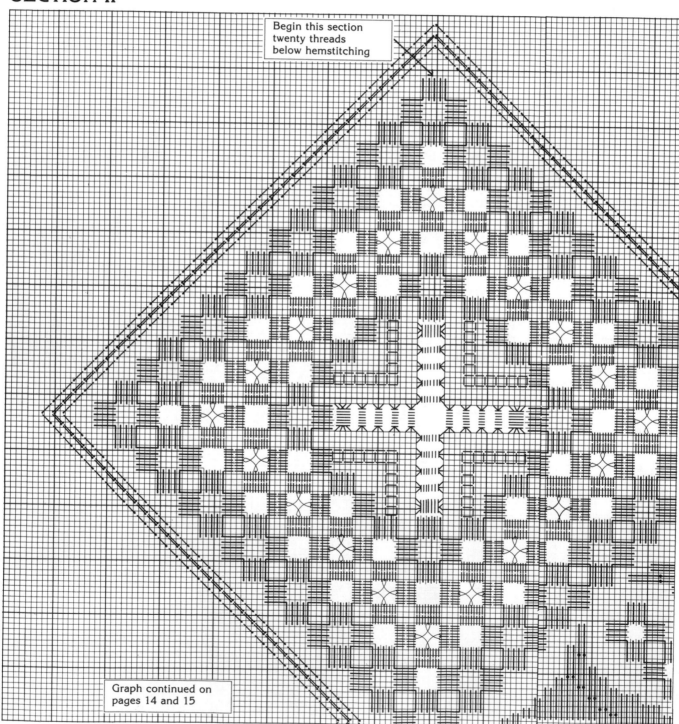

Begin this section
twenty threads
below hemstitching

Graph continued on
pages 14 and 15

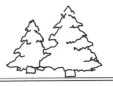

Center of design

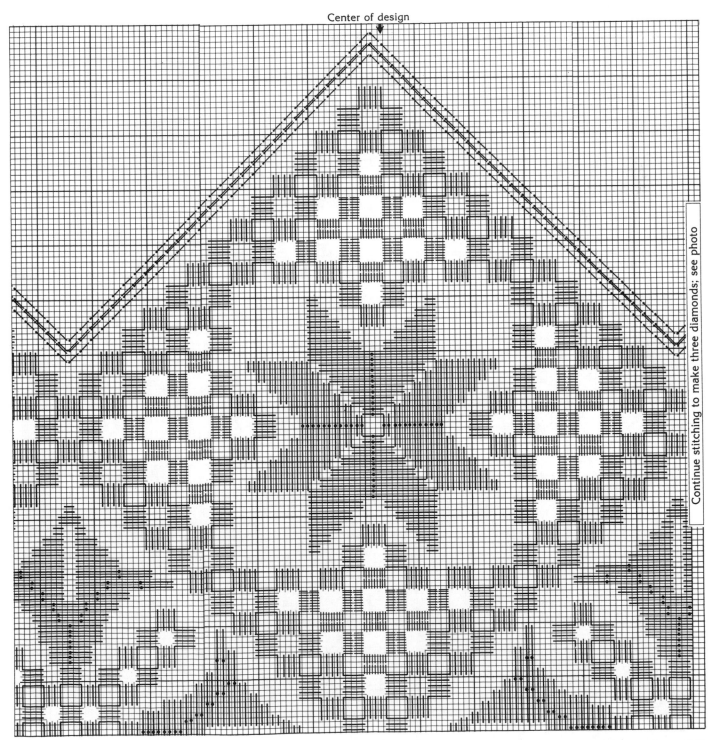

Continue stitching to make three diamonds; see photo

SECTION II continued from pages 12 and 13

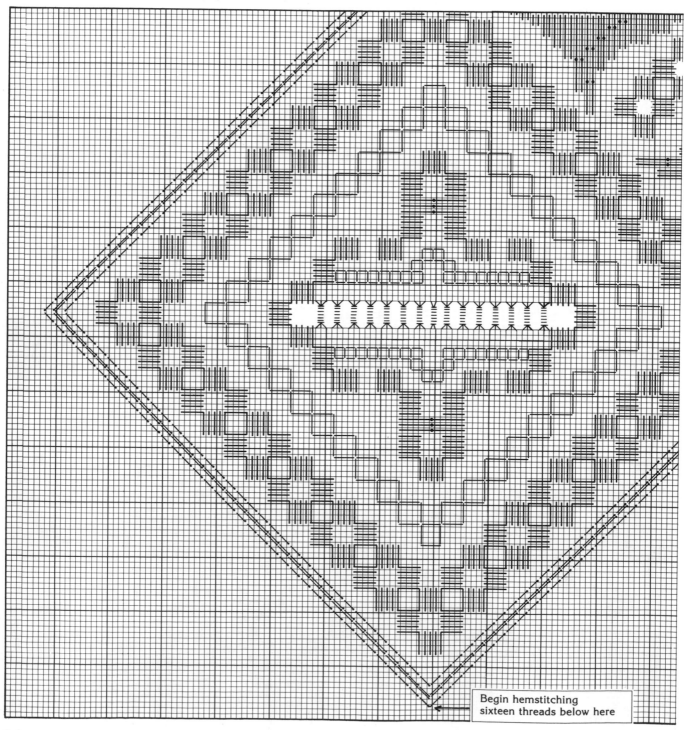

Begin hemstitching
sixteen threads below here

Center of design

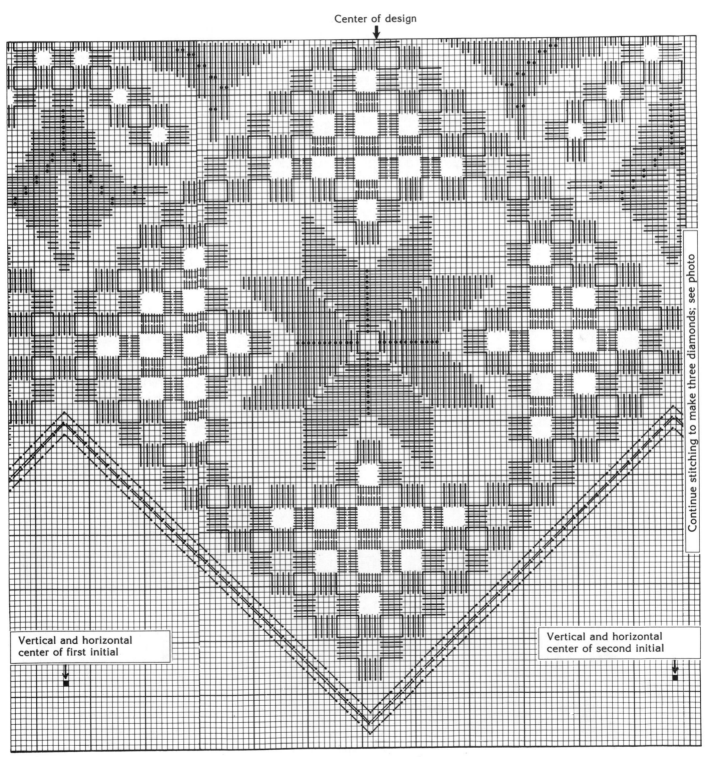

Continue stitching to make three diamonds; see photo

Vertical and horizontal
center of first initial

Vertical and horizontal
center of second initial

SECTION III

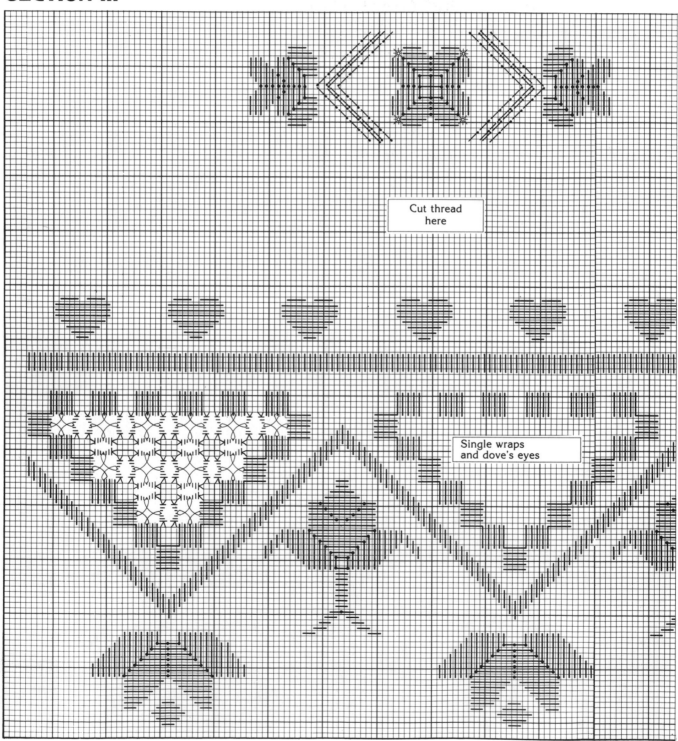

Cut thread here

Single wraps and dove's eyes

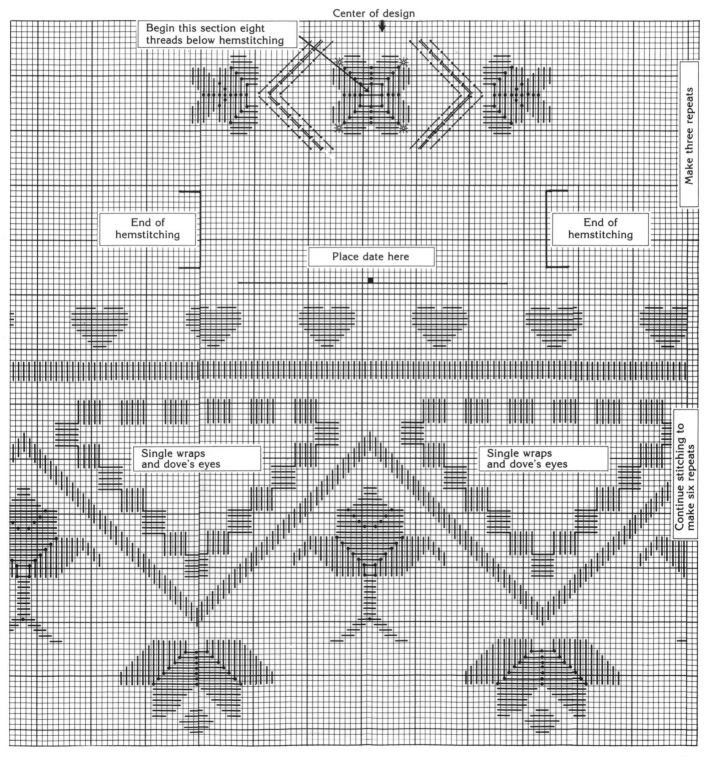

Center of design

Begin this section eight
threads below hemstitching

Make three repeats

End of
hemstitching

End of
hemstitching

Place date here

Single wraps
and dove's eyes

Single wraps
and dove's eyes

Continue stitching to
make six repeats

THE BEAUTY OF THIS PIECE is in the variety of stitches used to accent a repeated symmetry. Worked on evenweave fabric, this embroidery calls for simple stitches which create a complex design.

Begin by familiarizing yourself with the symbols on the graph and the names of the stitches. You may want to practice on a scrap of fabric. Each grid line on the graph represents one thread of linen. With Hardanger—another fabric you might use—each thread has two fibers that are counted as one.

When using the graph for all stitches except cross-stitch, count threads, not holes. In the cross-stitch on this piece, note that the initials are stitched over one thread and numerals over two.

The design is divided into three horizontal sections, and the place to begin each is marked. Work all of each section before proceeding to the next, and work all of each stitch in the order given.

For additional information about the stitches used in this design, refer to *The Complete DMC Encyclopedia of Needlework* by deDillmont or to "Teach Yourself Hardanger Embroidery" by Stockdale from Leisure Arts leaflet 330.

SECTION I

A. Surface Embroidery

1. **Kloster Blocks:** Stitch with one strand of Flower Thread #700. Complete all Kloster blocks in diamonds. A Kloster block is five satin stitches worked over four threads.

2. **Satin Stitch:** Stitch with one strand of DMC 822 Pearl Cotton #8. Complete both flower borders and centers of diamonds. Dots on graph indicate where needle goes down through fabric.

3. **Eyelet Stitch:** Stitch with one strand of DMC 644 embroidery floss over two threads. First, open an "eye" in fabric by spreading threads in center of stitch with a needle. Come up through "eye" and follow diagram for placement. Pull "eye" firmly with each stitch.

4. **Faggot Stitch:** Stitch with one strand of DMC 642 embroidery floss. Faggot-stitching is worked in two parallel rows, drawing up stitches firmly. Follow diagram closely, noting compensating stitch at each corner.

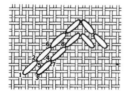

B. Needleweaving

1. **Single Wrap** and **Dove's Eye Stitch:** Stitch with one strand of DMC 644 embroidery floss in all diamonds except center diamond. Cut threads from area to be worked; note blank areas on graph. Wrap as many times as needed to cover threads entirely, making a bar. (Lines in symbol on graph are not meant to indicate number of wraps.) Make dove's eye once threads are wrapped on all four sides of a block; then move to next block.

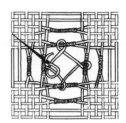

2. **Figure-eight** and **Dove's Eye Stitch:** Stitch with one strand of DMC 644 embroidery floss in center diamond. Cut threads from area to be worked. Weave over first two threads and under two; continue until bar is full. Complete dove's eye and move to next block.

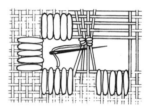

3. **Hemstitch** and **Openwork:** Stitch with one strand of DMC 644 embroidery floss. Begin top edge of hemstitching ten threads below flower border. Place bottom edge twelve threads below top edge. Pull threads. Hemstitch first top and then bottom of twelve-thread area to be stitched; stitch threads into groups of four. For openwork, cross threads with a single strand of floss, following diagram.

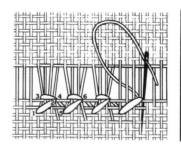

On this diagram only, one thread stands for four threads of fabric.

SECTION II

A. Surface Embroidery

1. **Kloster Blocks:** Stitch with one strand of Flower Thread #700. Begin top block twenty threads below hemstitching. Complete all Kloster blocks in diamonds.

2. **Satin Stitch:** Stitch with one strand of DMC 822 Pearl Cotton #8. Complete all satin-stitching in diamonds.

 3. **Double Faggot Stitch:** Stitch with one strand of DMC 642 embroidery floss. Work first round as with faggot-stitching above. For second round, bring needle up at 1 and down at 2; draw up stitch. Next bring needle up at C and down at D, overlapping thread from second row of first round. Return to bottom row and continue.

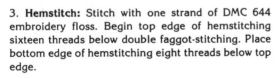

 4. **Box Stitch:** Stitch with one strand of DMC 642 embroidery floss in upper diamonds. Stitch with one strand of DMC 822 Pearl Cotton #8 in lower diamonds.

 5. **Cross-stitch:** Stitch with one strand of DMC 644 embroidery floss over one thread. (See General Instructions, page 6.) Complete both initials. Find center of initial on graph (pages 20-21); stitch center of initial over black box on graph.

B. Needleweaving

 1. **Single Wrap:** Stitch with one strand of DMC 644 embroidery floss.

 2. **Figure-eight** and **Dove's Eye Stitch:** Stitch with one strand of DMC 644 embroidery floss.

3. **Hemstitch:** Stitch with one strand of DMC 644 embroidery floss. Begin top edge of hemstitching sixteen threads below double faggot-stitching. Place bottom edge of hemstitching eight threads below top edge.

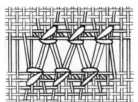

SECTION III

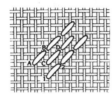 ### A. Surface Embroidery

1. **Satin Stitch:** Stitch with one strand of DMC 822 Pearl Cotton #8. Complete three flower motifs.

 2. **Eyelet Stitch:** Stitch with one strand of DMC 644 embroidery floss over one thread.

 3. **Double Faggot Stitch:** Stitch with one strand of DMC 642 embroidery floss.

 4. **Cross-stitch:** Stitch with two strands of DMC 642 embroidery floss over two threads. (See General Instructions, page 6.) Transfer numerals (page 96) to graph paper with two threads (one stitch) between. Mark horizontal center and stitch on line indicated for date on graph.

B. Needleweaving

1. **Hemstitch:** Stitch with one strand of DMC 644 embroidery floss.

Plan inside ends of hemstitched areas to be ½" from cross-stitched date. Cut twelve threads near center of each area. Remove threads from outermost halves. Working from back of fabric, remove threads from center-cut to inside ends of areas. Place one thread at a time in tapestry needle and weave under warp threads for ½". Trim ends. Complete hemstitching to make groups of four threads, then divide and cross threads.

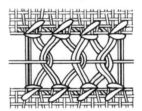

 ### C. Surface embroidery

1. **Satin Stitch:** Stitch hearts with one strand of DMC 822 Pearl Cotton #8.

 2. **Satin Stitch:** Stitch straight border with one strand of Flower Thread #700.

 3. **Kloster Blocks:** Stitch with one strand of Flower Thread #700.

 4. **Satin Stitch:** Stitch zig-zag border with one strand of Flower Thread #700.

 5. **Satin Stitch:** Stitch flowers with one strand of DMC 822 Pearl Cotton #8.

 ### D. Needleweaving

1. **Single Wrap** and **Daisy Stitch:** Stitch with one strand of DMC 644 embroidery floss, pulling dove's eyes somewhat tighter than above to make "daisies."

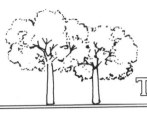

THE CHANGING SEASONS

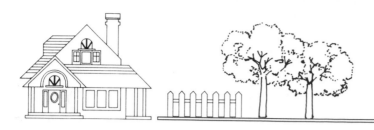

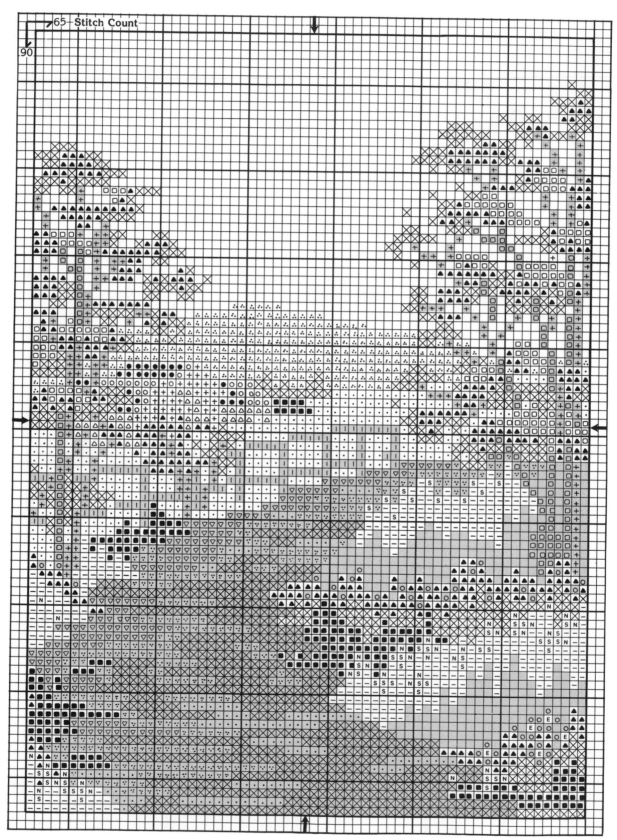

65 Stitch Count

90

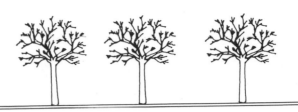

65 Stitch Count

90

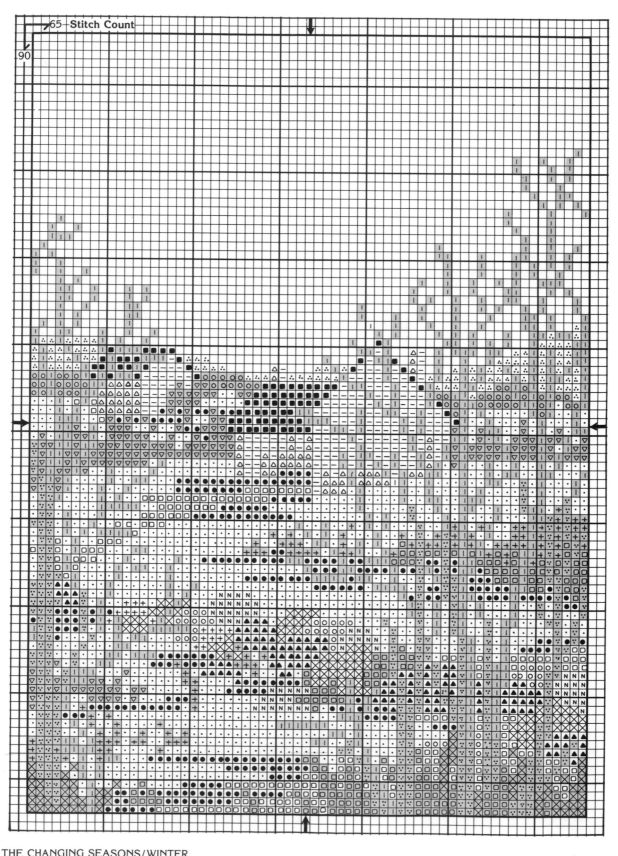

65 Stitch Count

190

May each season bring with it a new beginning.

SPRING

Bates		DMC (used for model)
	Step 1:	Cross-stitch (two strands)
1	+	White
293	◉	727 Topaz-vy lt.
323	+	722 Orange Spice-lt.
117	▽	341 Blue Violet-lt.
119	✕	333 Blue Violet-dk.
264	·	772 Pine Green-lt.
242	−	989 Forest Green
244	◉	987 Forest Green-dk.
213	▣	369 Pistachio Green-vy lt.
214	✕	368 Pistachio Green-lt.
215	▪	320 Pistachio Green-med.
215	▲	320 Pistachio Green-dk.
875	∴	503 Blue Green-med.
363	▣	436 Tan
339	● ╱	920 Copper-med.
378	▯	841 Beige Brown-lt.
379	⁛	840 Beige Brown-med.
397	▲	762 Pearl Gray-vy. lt.
	Step 2:	Backstitch (one strand)
905	⌐	645 Beaver Gray-vy. dk.

SUMMER

Bates		DMC (used for model)
	Step 1:	Cross-stitch (two strands)
1	+	White
293	·	727 Topaz-vy lt.
295	E	726 Topaz-lt.
316	◎	740 Tangerine

Bates		DMC (used for model)
335	s	606 Orange Red-bright
19	N	817 Coral Red-vy. dk.
875	∴	503 Blue Green-med.
842	▨	3013 Khaki Green-lt.
265	▯	3348 Yellow Green-lt.
266	✕	3347 Yellow Green-med.
243	▲	988 Forest Green-med.
265	−	471 Avocado Green-vy. lt.
267	▪	469 Avocado Green
216	▨	367 Pistachio Green-dk.
362	+	437 Tan-lt.
363	⁛	436 Tan
309	▯	435 Brown-vy. lt.
370	✕	434 Brown-lt.
378	▮	841 Beige Brown-lt.
347	▽	402 Mahogany-vy. lt.
339	◦	920 Copper-med.
5968	●	355 Terra Cotta-dk.
397	△	762 Pearl Gray-vy. lt.
	Step 2:	Backstitch (one strand)
905	⌐	645 Beaver Gray-vy. dk.

FALL

Bates		DMC (used for model)
	Step 1:	Cross-stitch (two strands)
886	+	667 Old Gold-vy. lt.
891	·	676 Old Gold-lt.
890	◦	729 Old Gold-med.
901	▲	680 Old Gold-dk.
307	✕	783 Christmas Gold

Bates	Symbol	DMC	Color
306	□	725	Topaz
324	I	721	Orange Spice-med.
326	▽	720	Orange Spice-dk.
337	–	922	Copper-lt.
339	■	920	Copper-med.
875	∴	503	Blue Green-med.
266	△	471	Avocado Green-vy. lt.
267	●	469	Avocado Green
942	N	738	Tan-vy. lt.
363	E	436	Tan
309	O	435	Brown-vy. lt.
355	╳	975	Golden Brown-dk.
903	∵	3032	Mocha Brown-med.
900	+	3024	Brown Gray-vy. lt.
8581	□	647	Beaver Gray-med.

Step 2: Backstitch (one strand)

Bates	Symbol	DMC	Color
905	backstitch line	645	Beaver Gray-vy. dk.

WINTER

Bates **DMC** (used for model)

Step 1: Cross-stitch (two strands)

Bates	Symbol	DMC	Color
886	–	677	Old Gold-vy. lt.
159	●	827	Blue-vy. lt.
120	□	794	Cornflower Blue-lt.
849	O	927	Slate Green-med.
875	∴	503	Blue Green-med.
942	△	738	Tan-vy. lt.
363	▽	436	Tan
882	+	407	Sportsman Flesh-dk.
5975	□	356	Terra Cotta-med.
5968	╳	355	Terra Cotta-dk.
339	■	920	Copper-med.
903	N	3032	Mocha Brown-med.
378	I	841	Beige Brown-lt.
379	∵	840	Beige Brown-med.
397	·	762	Pearl Gray-vy. lt.
398	O	453	Shell Gray-lt.
900	+	3024	Brown Gray-vy. lt.
8581	╳	647	Beaver Gray-med.
905	▲	645	Beaver Gray-vy. dk.

Step 2: Backstitch (one strand)

Bates	Symbol	DMC	Color
905	backstitch line	645	Beaver Gray-vy. dk.

MODELS Stitch on cream Linda 27 over two threads. The finished design size is 4¾″ × 6⅝″. Cut the Linda 29″ × 14″. Finished design sizes for other fabrics are Aida 11—5⅞″ × 8⅛″; Aida 14—4⅝″ × 6⅜″; Aida 18—3⅝″ × 5″; Hardanger 22—3″ × 4⅛″.

MODEL for table runner Stitch on cream Salem Cloth 14. Cut the fabric 14½″ × 36½″ or to fit your table. Stitch the motif in one corner of the fabric 1¼″ from each edge. Repeat the motif along the 36½″ edge until the design fills the length of the fabric which will hang over the edge of the table. Repeat along the second 36½″ edge of the fabric; use the photo as a guide. To finish, fray the edges of the fabric by removing six strands or about ⅜″.

MODEL for bread cover Stitch on cream Salem Cloth 14. The finished design size for one motif is 6″ × 2½″. Cut the fabric 19″ × 19″ or to fit your favorite basket. Stitch two motifs in one corner of the fabric about ¼″ apart, with each motif about 1″ and 2½″ from the edges of the fabric; use the photo as a guide. To finish, fray the edges of the fabric by removing six strands or about ⅜″. Finished design sizes for one motif stitched on other fabrics are Aida 11—7⅝″ × 3⅛″; Aida 14—6″ × 2½″; Aida 18—4⅝″ × 2″; Hardanger 22—3⅞″ × 1⅝″.

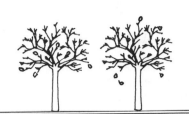

Bates		DMC (used for model)
	Step 1:	Cross-stitch (two strands)
295	●	726 Topaz-lt.
306	⊙	725 Topaz
323	✕	722 Orange Spice-lt.
324	○	721 Orange Spice-med.
11	▲	3328 Salmon-med.
882	▯	407 Sportsman Flesh-dk.
5975	⊠	356 Terra Cotta-med.
869	▢	3042 Antique Violet-lt.
920	⊡	932 Antique Blue-lt.
168	▽	597 Turquoise

Bates		DMC
186	▢	993 Aquamarine-lt.
264	·	772 Pine Green-lt.
253	∴	472 Avocado Green-ultra lt.
203	–	954 Nile Green
256	△	704 Chartreuse-bright
239	■	702 Kelly Green
	Step 2:	Backstitch (one strand)
11	⌐	3328 Salmon-med. (orange leaf)
5975	⌐	356 Terra Cotta-med. (brown leaf)
168	⌐	597 Turquoise (blue leaf)
239	⌐	702 Kelly Green (green leaf)

84-Stitch Count
35

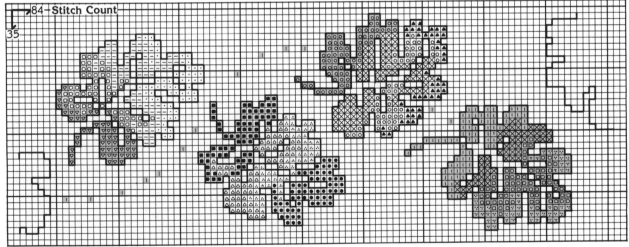

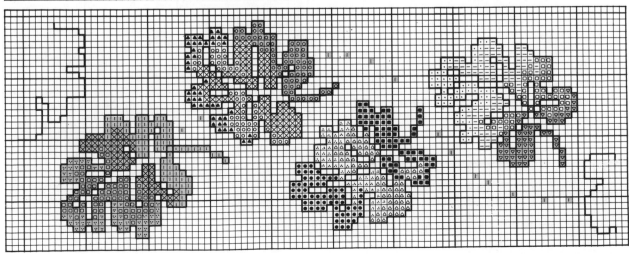

. . . your pride of place in family history.

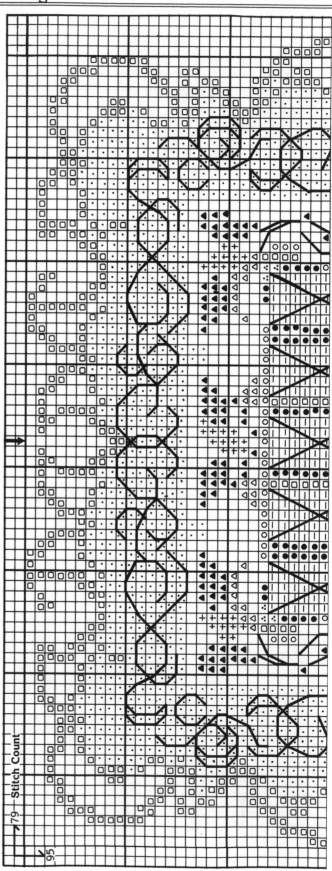

See code on page 49.

To personalize this sampler, graph the name on a separate sheet of paper and center it in the space provided.

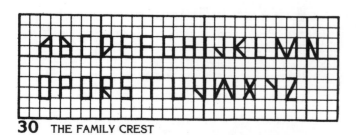

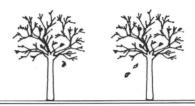

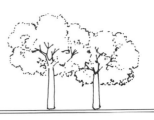

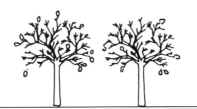

SEE GRAPH ON PAGE 60

44 SEE GRAPH ON PAGE 79

SHHH! BABY'S SLEEPING

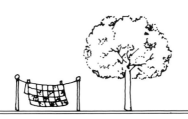

See graph on page 30.

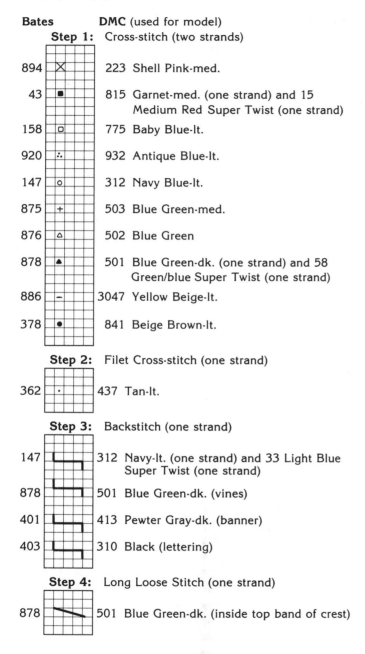

Bates		DMC (used for model)
	Step 1:	Cross-stitch (two strands)
894	×	223 Shell Pink-med.
43	■	815 Garnet-med. (one strand) and 15 Medium Red Super Twist (one strand)
158	□	775 Baby Blue-lt.
920	∴	932 Antique Blue-lt.
147	○	312 Navy Blue-lt.
875	+	503 Blue Green-med.
876	△	502 Blue Green
878	▲	501 Blue Green-dk. (one strand) and 58 Green/blue Super Twist (one strand)
886	–	3047 Yellow Beige-lt.
378	●	841 Beige Brown-lt.
	Step 2:	Filet Cross-stitch (one strand)
362	·	437 Tan-lt.
	Step 3:	Backstitch (one strand)
147		312 Navy-lt. (one strand) and 33 Light Blue Super Twist (one strand)
878		501 Blue Green-dk. (vines)
401		413 Pewter Gray-dk. (banner)
403		310 Black (lettering)
	Step 4:	Long Loose Stitch (one strand)
878		501 Blue Green-dk. (inside top band of crest)

MODEL Stitch on cream Belfast Linen 32 over two threads. The finished design size is 5″ × 6″. Cut the fabric 11″ × 12″. Finished design sizes for other fabrics are Aida 11—7⅛″ × 8⅝″; Aida 14—5⅝″ × 6¾″; Aida 18—4⅜″ × 5¼″; Hardanger 22—3⅝″ × 4⅜″. Madeira Super Twist #30 is available to shop owners from Treadleart, 25834-1 Narbonne Avenue, Lomita, CA 90717.

... from the seed catalog,
to the garden,
to your kitchen table!

THE ORCHARD

Bates			DMC (used for model)
		Step 1:	Cross-stitch (two strands)
292	×	◢	3078 Golden Yellow-vy. lt.
48	–	◢	818 Baby Pink
25	+		3326 Rose-lt.
66	E	◢	3688 Mauve-med.
42	△		309 Rose-deep
158	·	◢	747 Sky Blue-vy. lt.
167	∴	◢	519 Sky Blue
162	■		517 Wedgewood-med.
186	□		993 Aquamarine-lt.
189	●		991 Aquamarine-dk.
362	○		437 Tan-lt.
370	▲		434 Brown-lt.
		Step 2:	Backstitch (one strand)
186			993 Aquamarine-lt. (flower stems)
189			991 Aquamarine-dk. (cherry stems)
370			434 Brown-lt. (apple stems, birds' feet)
905			645 Beaver Gray-vy. dk. (birds)

MODEL Stitch on white Aida 14. The finished design size is 4⅞″ × 6¾″. Cut the fabric 11″ × 13″. Finished design sizes for other fabrics are Aida 11—6⅛″ × 8⅝″; Aida 18—3¾″ × 5¼″; Hardanger 22—3⅛″ × 4⅜″. Information about the silk-screened mats in the photo is available from Chapelle Designers. Send a self-addressed, stamped envelope to Chapelle Designers, Box 9252 Newgate Station, Ogden, Utah 84409.

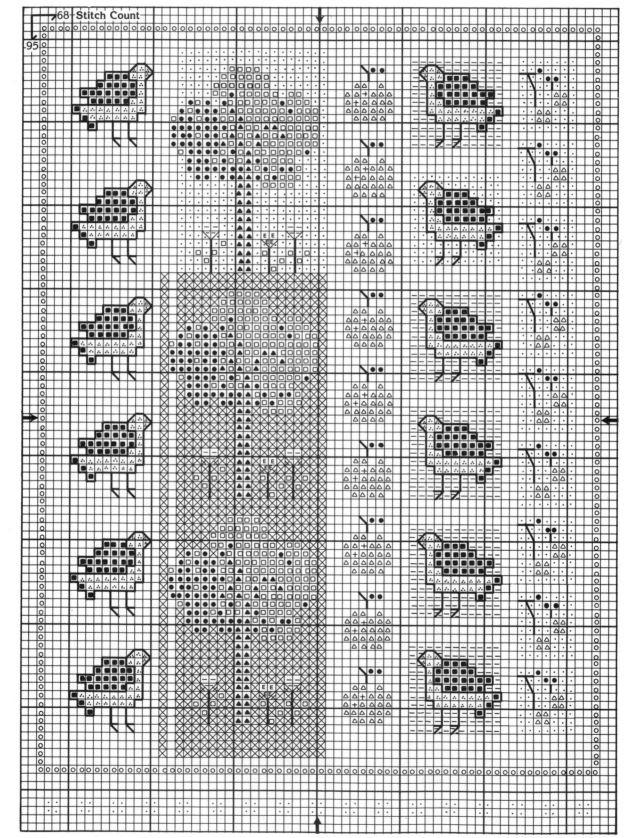

68 Stitch Count

95

THE VILLAGE

Bates		DMC (used for model)	
Step 1:		Cross-stitch (two strands)	
1	∴ ◿		White
292	·	3078	Golden Yellow-vy. lt.
891	K	676	Old Gold-lt.
66	U	3688	Mauve-med.
897	◔	221	Shell Pink-dk.
117	+	341	Blue Violet-lt.
119	▫	333	Blue Violet-dk.
167	s	519	Sky Blue
147	N	312	Navy Blue-lt.
206	–	955	Nile Green-lt.
203	✕ ◿	954	Nile Green
209	●	913	Nile Green-med.
186	△	993	Aquamarine-lt.
187	H	992	Aquamarine
189	▲	991	Aquamarine-dk.
362	z	437	Tan-lt.
370	E	434	Brown-lt.
905	■	645	Beaver Gray-vy. dk.

Bates		DMC	
Step 2:		Backstitch (one strand)	
66		3688	Mauve-med. (broken lines)
189		991	Aquamarine-dk. (rabbits)
905		645	Beaver Gray-vy. dk. (houses)

MODEL Stitch on white Aida 14. The finished design size is 4⅞″ × 6⅝″. Cut the fabric 11″ × 13″. Finished design sizes for other fabrics are Aida 11—6⅛″ × 8½″; Aida 18—3¾″ × 5⅛″; Hardanger 22—3⅛″ × 4¼″. Information about the silk-screened mats in the photo is available from Chapelle Designers. Send a self-addressed, stamped envelope to Chapelle Designers, Box 9252 Newgate Station, Ogden, Utah 84409.

THE FARMER

Bates		DMC (used for model)	
Step 1:		Cross-stitch (two strands)	
1	∴ ◿		White
292	△	3078	Golden Yellow-vy. lt.
324	▲	922	Copper-lt.
894	▫	223	Shell Pink-med.
897	s	221	Shell Pink-dk.
158	· ◿	747	Sky Blue-vy. lt.
167	■	519	Sky Blue
147	E	312	Navy Blue-lt.
242	○ ◿	989	Forest Green
186	+ ◿	993	Aquamarine-lt.
189	● ◢	991	Aquamarine-dk.
942	– ◿	738	Tan-vy. lt.
362	✕ ◿	437	Tan-lt.
370	z	434	Brown-lt.
905	N	645	Beaver Gray-vy. dk.

Bates		DMC	
Step 2:		Backstitch (one strand)	
147		312	Navy Blue-lt. (rabbit, clothing)
189		991	Aquamarine-dk. (vegetables)
905		645	Beaver Gray-vy. dk. (all else)

MODEL Stitch on white Aida 14. The finished design size is 4⅞″ × 6⅝″. Cut the fabric 11″ × 13″. Finished design sizes for other fabrics are Aida 11—6⅛″ × 8½″; Aida 18—3¾″ × 5⅛″; Hardanger 22—3⅛″ × 4¼″. Information about the silk-screened mats in the photo is available from Chapelle Designers. Send a self-addressed, stamped envelope to Chapelle Designers, Box 9252 Newgate Station, Ogden, Utah 84409.

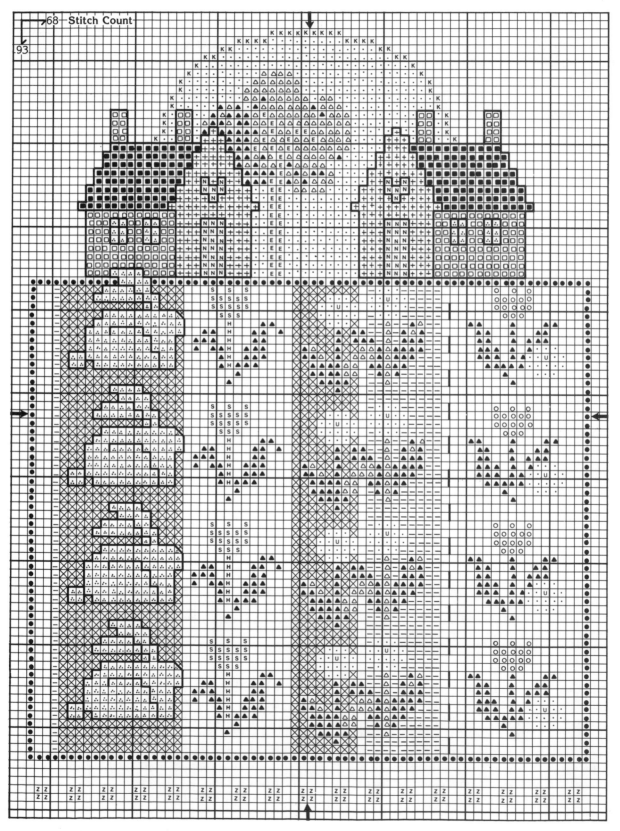

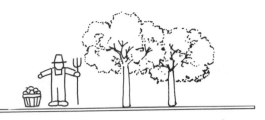

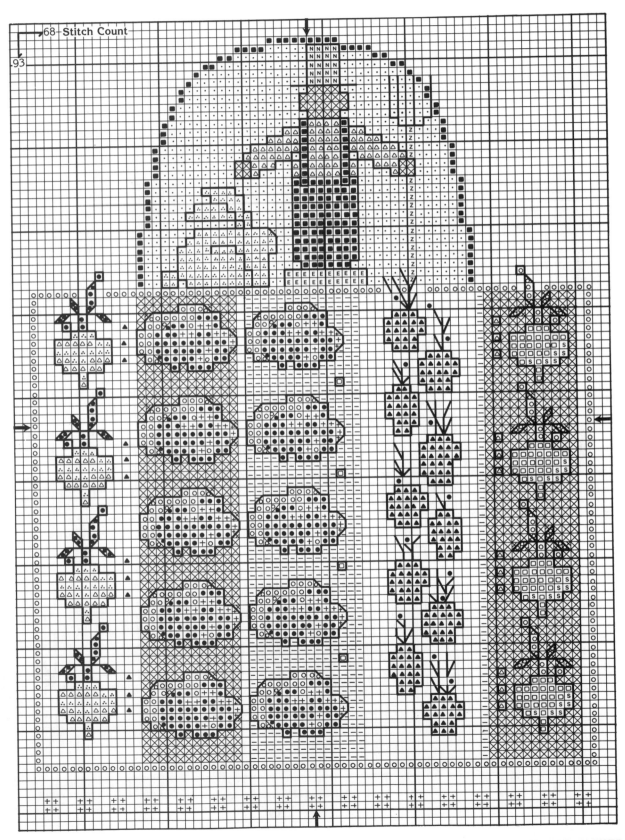

68—Stitch Count

93

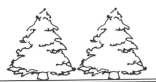

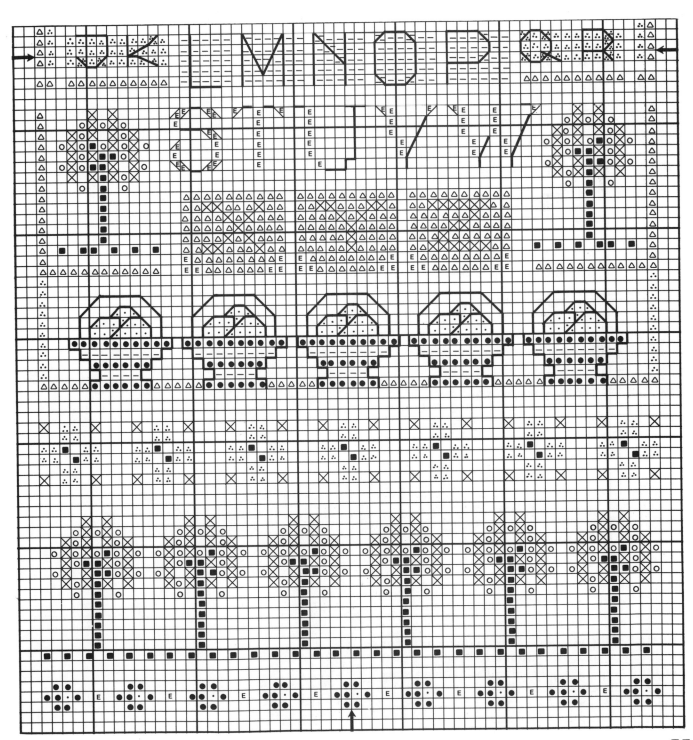

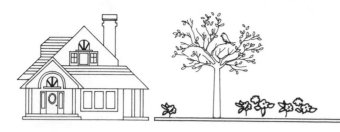

Bates			DMC (used for model)
		Step 1:	Cross-stitch (two strands)
887	· /	3046	Yellow Beige-med.
307	+	783	Christmas Gold
333	s /	900	Burnt Orange-dk.
339	▲	920	Copper-med.
44	■	814	Garnet-dk.
921	∴	931	Antique Blue-med.
149	✕ /	311	Navy Blue-med.
844	△	3012	Khaki Green-med.
846	E /	3051	Green Gray-dk.
246	o /	319	Pistachio Green-vy. dk.
373	−	422	Hazel Nut Brown-lt.
882	▫	407	Sportsman Flesh-dk.
936	● /	632	Negro Flesh

		Step 2:	Backstitch (one strand)
44		814	Garnet-dk. (poles, J through R)
149		311	Navy Blue-med. (rooster, eggs, B, D, F, G, H, I)
846		3051	Green Gray-dk. (vines, boxes, S through W)
246		319	Pistachio Green-vy. dk. (numbers, A, C, E)
936		632	Negro Flesh (basket handles)

		Step 3:	French Knots (one strand)
149	●	311	Navy Blue-med.

Up you go! Breakfast is ready, Grandma and Grandpa are already at the table.

MODEL Stitch on light brown Linen 25 over two threads. The finished design size is 4¾″ × 10⅛″. Cut the fabric 11″ × 17″. Finished design sizes for other fabrics are Aida 11—5½″ × 11½″; Aida 14—4¼″ × 9″; Aida 18—3⅜″ × 7″; Hardanger 22—2¾″ × 5¾″.

... a personal retreat,
a place to escape daily rituals.
Curl up with a good book
or write an overdue letter.

Step 2: Backstitch (one strand)

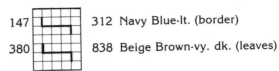

Bates		312 Navy Blue-lt. (border)
147		312 Navy Blue-lt. (border)
380		838 Beige Brown-vy. dk. (leaves)

MODEL Stitch on cream Belfast Linen 32 over two threads. The finished design size is 4⅝″ × 10⅝″. Cut the fabric 11″ × 17″. Finished design sizes for other fabrics are Aida 11—6¾″ × 15½″; Aida 14—5¼″ × 12⅛″; Aida 18—4⅛″ × 9½″; Hardanger 22—3⅜″ × 7¾″.

Bates   **DMC** (used for model)
     Step 1: Cross-stitch (two strands)

Bates		DMC
886	–	677 Old Gold-vy. lt.
891	E	676 Old Gold-lt.
307	+	977 Golden Brown-lt.
324	△	721 Orange Spice-med.
326	s	720 Orange Spice-dk.
11	∴	350 Coral-med.
19	✕	817 Coral Red-vy. dk.
20	▲	498 Christmas Red-dk.
969	▽	316 Antique Mauve-med.
970	▨	315 Antique Mauve-dk.
158	∷	775 Baby Blue-lt.
159	I	3325 Baby Blue
145	▢	334 Baby Blue-med.
147	✕	312 Navy Blue-lt.
842	◉	3013 Khaki Green-lt.
349	·	921 Copper
339	○	920 Copper-med.
341	N	919 Red Copper
5975	▫	356 Terra Cotta-med.
5968	●	355 Terra Cotta-dk.
936	■	632 Negro Flesh

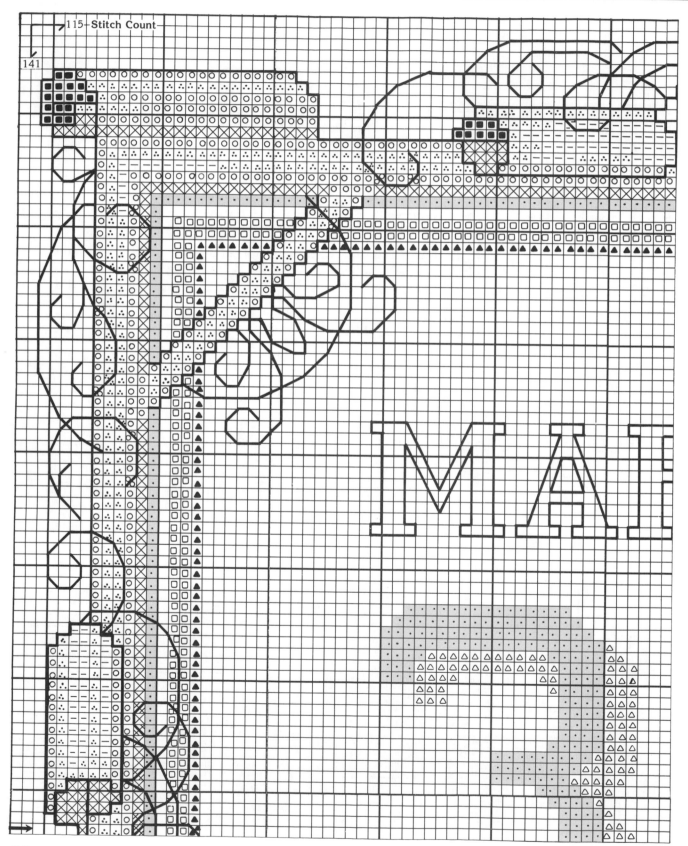

115–Stitch Count

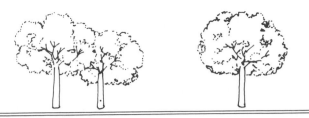

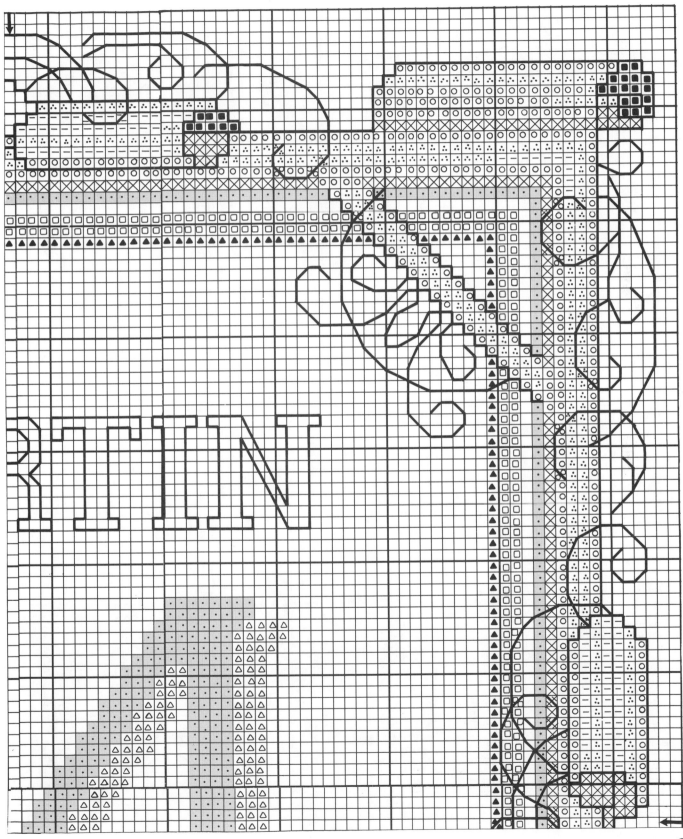

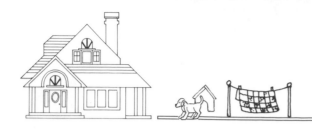

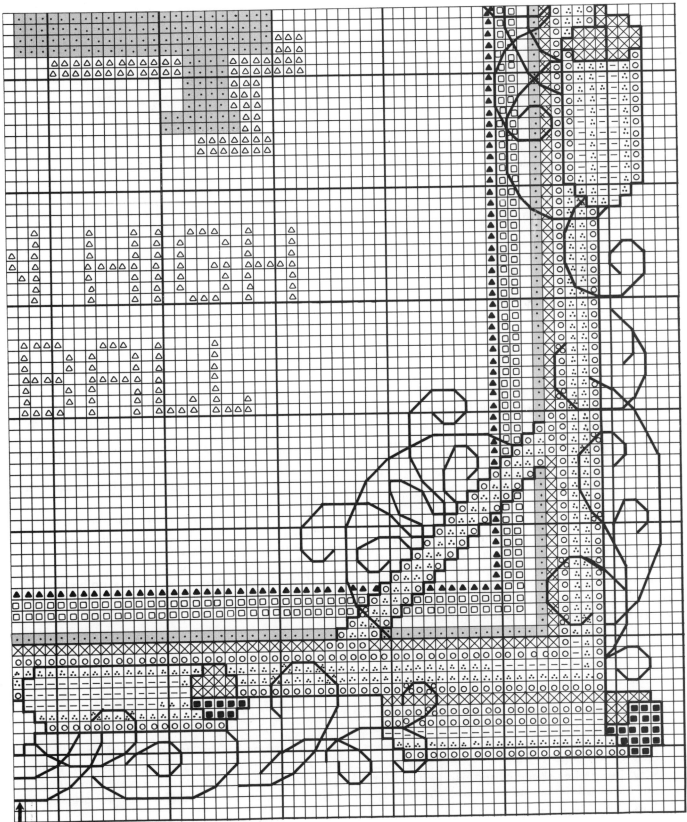

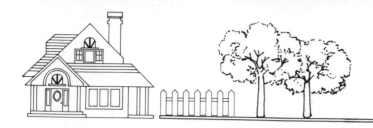

Bates		DMC (used for model)
	Step 1:	Cross-stitch (two strands)
292	−	3078 Golden Yellow-vy. lt.
886	∴	677 Old Gold-vy. lt.
891	○	676 Old Gold-lt.
890	✕	729 Old Gold-med.
901	■	680 Old Gold-dk.
887	▫	372 Mustard-lt.
889	▲	370 Mustard-med.
161	▪	826 Blue-med.
164	△	824 Blue-vy. dk.
	Step 2:	Backstitch (one strand)
164		824 Blue-vy. dk. (lettering)
370		434 Brown-lt. (all else)

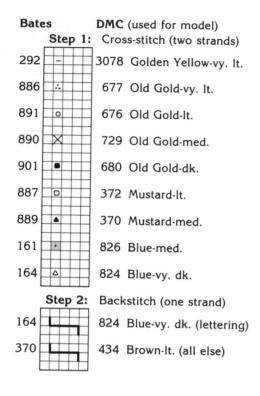

For the one who recalls moments of victory and defeat, laughter and tears...

MODEL Stitch on cream Aida 14. The finished design size is 8¼″ × 10⅛″. Cut the fabric 15″ × 17″. Finished design sizes for other fabrics are Aida 11—10½″ × 12⅞″; Aida 18—6⅜″ × 7⅞″; Hardanger 22—5¼″ × 6⅜″.

The model was stitched for a young athlete who wears a blue jersey. But unless your favorite football team's color is blue, you will want to personalize this sampler with special colors.

In the chart below, the designer lists the specific DMC floss colors she suggests you use. As she picked these colors, she placed the skeins of floss next to the golds of the border to make sure the new colors would work nicely with the border. You will want to do the same if you are thinking of using floss colors that are different from the designer's suggestions in the chart.

Here are some examples of personalizing the sampler with color:

If the team's color is red, replace DMC 824 and 826 in the code with 815 and 817, respectively. This way, the darker shade of red will be used for the shadow of the jersey number, and the lighter shade will be used for the number itself.

If the team's colors are red and white, use DMC 815 and 817, and stitch the design on white fabric instead of cream fabric.

If the team's colors are black and orange, use the lighter color (orange) for the jersey number, referring to the chart below. Use the darker color (black) for the lettering.

Use your team spirit, your imagination, and your good taste, and you're guaranteed to create an heirloom!

Team Color	DMC Numbers (shadow color listed first)
Green	986, 988
Purple	550, 327
Orange	720, 721
Red	815, 817
Maroon	902, 815
Black	Black, 645

To personalize the graph, refer to the alphabets and numerals on pages 65-66. Center the jersey number and the names of the player and the school in the space available; see the graph for placement.

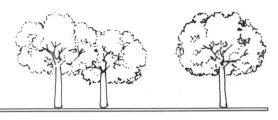

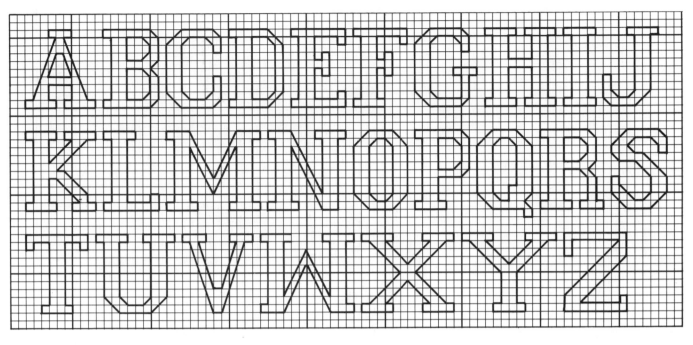

Bed and breakfast are all
your guests expect.
Love and caring are what
you have to give.

Bates		DMC (used for model)	
Step 1:		Cross-stitch (two strands)	
95	■	554	Violet-lt.
117	△	341	Blue Violet-lt.
158	−	828	Blue Ultra-vy. lt.
130	· ╱	799	Delft-med.
264	□	772	Pine Green-lt.
214	✕	966	Baby Green-med.
216	▲	367	Pistachio Green-dk.
830	○	644	Beige Gray-med.
392	●	642	Beige Gray-dk.
Step 2:		Backstitch (one strand)	
147		312	Navy Blue-lt. (flowers, center alphabet)
392		642	Beige Gray-dk. (top alphabet, around O, U, X in center alphabet
216		367	Pistachio Green-dk. (all else)
Step 3:		Beadwork	
	∴		Amethyst (MPR 520)

MODEL for sampler Stitch on cream Belfast Linen 32 over two threads. The finished design size is 6¾" × 9⅛". Cut the fabric 13" × 16". Finished design sizes for other fabrics are Aida 11—9⅞" × 13¼"; Aida 14—7¾" × 10⅜"; Aida 18—6" × 8⅛"; Hardanger 22—4⅞" × 6⅝".

MATERIALS for one sachet Completed cross-stitch on cream Belfast Linen 32—see model information; one 5" × 5" piece of unstitched cream Belfast Linen 32 and matching thread; 1⅛ yards of 1¾"-wide cream lace trim; ⅜ yard of ⅜"-wide cream flat lace; 2 tablespoons of potpourri; stuffing.

DIRECTIONS Divide the lace trim into quarters and mark. Stitch gathering threads close to the straight edge of the lace trim. Match the marks to the corners of the design piece; gather to fit. Pin the lace trim to the right side of the design piece with the straight edge of the lace matching the raw edges of the fabric. Stitch with a ¼" seam.

Place the right sides of the design piece and the unstitched linen together. Stitch on the stitching line for the lace, leaving an opening. Turn; stuff moderately and add the potpourri. Slipstitch the opening closed.

Fold the flat lace into 2½"-wide loops and tack to the sachet; see the photo for placement.

MATERIALS for dresser scarf Completed cross-stitch on cream Belfast Linen 32—see model information; 3⅛ yards of 1¾"-wide cream lace trim and matching thread; 4¼ yards of ⅜"-wide cream flat lace.

DIRECTIONS Cut the linen 23" × 18" with the design in one corner 4" from the edges. Fold ¼" double to the back of the scarf along the raw edges of the linen; stitch the hem. Pin the lace trim to the right side of the linen with the straight edge of the lace ¼" inside the finished edges of the scarf, allowing fullness at the corners. Stitch close to the straight edge of the lace.

Cut the flat lace in half. Place one length over the straight edge of the lace trim and slipstitch both edges to the scarf. Slipstitch both edges of the second length of flat lace to the scarf ⅛" inside the first length.

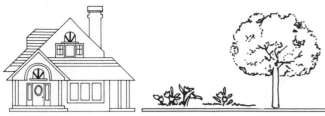

108-Stitch Count

146

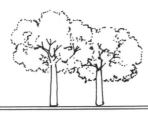

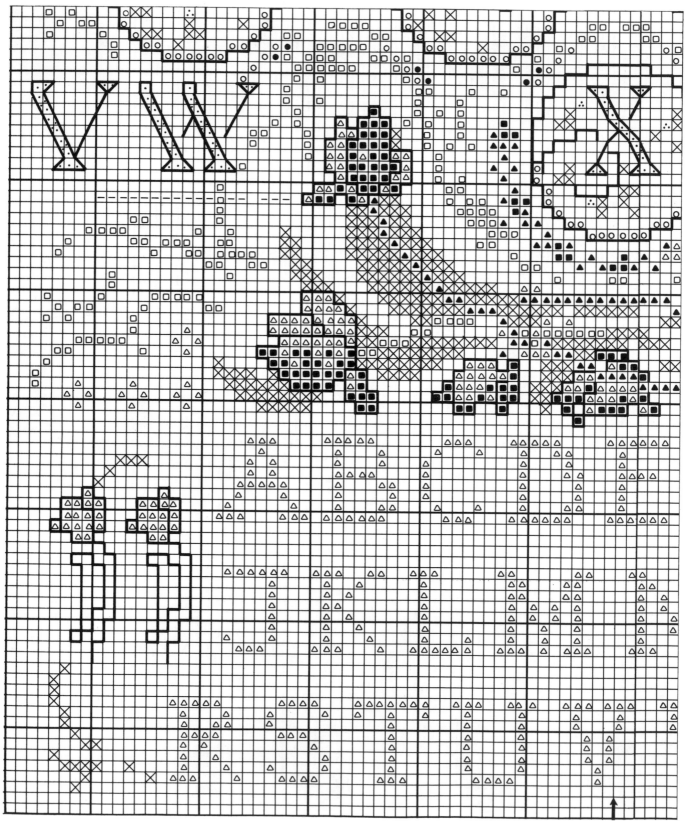

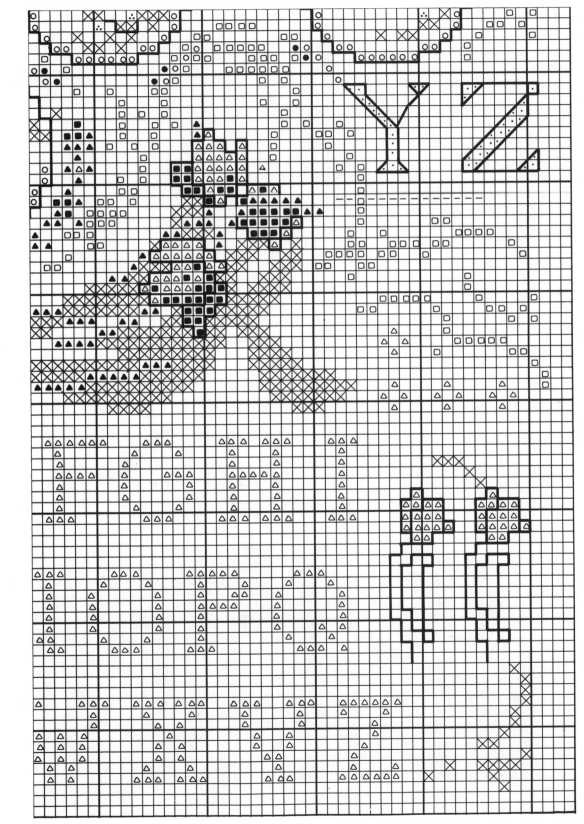

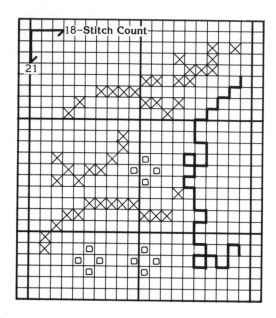

18-Stitch Count

21

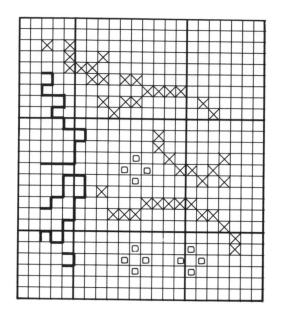

Bates		DMC (used for model)
Step 1:		Cross-stitch (two strands)
95	·	554 Violet-lt.
117	□	341 Blue Violet-lt.
264	✕	772 Pine Green-lt. (end motifs)
214	△	966 Baby Green-med.
216	✕	367 Pistachio Green-dk. (wreath motif)
392	–	642 Beige Gray-dk.
Step 2:		Backstitch (one strand)
216	∟	367 Pistachio Green-dk.
Step 3:		French Knots (one strand)
216	●	367 Pistachio Green-dk.

MODELS for pillow shams

Stitch on a purchased cream pillow sham using Waste Canvas 14. The finished design size for one end motif is 1¼″ × 1½″. Cut the waste canvas 10″ × 4″ for a design of three wreaths. Center the design parallel to and ¾″ from one end of the pillow sham. Finished design sizes for end motif stitched on other fabrics are
Aida 11—1⅝″ × 1⅞″; Aida 14—1¼″ × 1½″; Aida 18—1″ × 1⅛″; Hardanger 22—⅞″ × 1″.

MODELS for dresser scarf and sachet

Stitch on cream Belfast Linen 32 over two threads. The finished design size is 1½″ × 1½″. For the dresser scarf, cut the fabric 26″ × 21″; stitch the design 6″ from the right and bottom edges. For each sachet, cut the fabric 7″ × 7″; center the design. Finished design sizes for wreath stitched on other fabrics are
Aida 11—2¼″ × 2⅛″; Aida 14—1¾″ × 1¾″; Aida 18—1⅜″ × 1⅜″; Hardanger 22—1⅛″ × 1⅛″.

25-Stitch Count

24

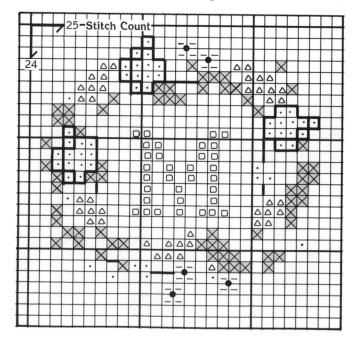

A SUMMER BREEZE

Simply stitch your
honest spirit —
a spirit that is winsome,
loving and sincere.

Bates			DMC (used for model)
Step 1:			**Cross-stitch (two strands)**
4146	▲		950 Sportsman Flesh-lt.
49	-	╱	3689 Mauve-lt.
24	s		776 Pink-med.
27	E		899 Rose-med.
104	▽	╱	210 Lavender-med.
105	∴	╱	209 Lavender-dk.
871	■	◢	3041 Antique Violet-med.
928	○		519 Sky Blue
167	✕		598 Turquoise-lt.
120	▨	╱	794 Cornflower Blue-lt.
121	△	╱	793 Cornflower Blue-med.
940	⋰		792 Cornflower Blue-dk.
213	◻	╱	369 Pistachio Green-vy. lt.
214	N		966 Baby Green-med.
206	◻		955 Nile Green-lt.
875	✕	◢	503 Blue Green-med.
189	●	◣	991 Aquamarine-dk.
392	▮		642 Beige Gray-dk.
903	◘		640 Beige Gray-vy. dk.
Step 2:			**Filet Cross-stitch (one strand)**
386	·	╱	746 Off White
Step 3:			**Backstitch (one strand)**
147	⌐		312 Navy Blue-lt.

Step 4:		**French Knots (one strand)**
147	●	312 Navy Blue-lt.
Step 5:		**Beadwork**
	■	Coral (MPR 275)

MODEL for sampler Stitch on white Dublin 25 over two threads. The finished design size is 9⅝″ × 9½″. Cut the fabric 16″ × 16″. Finished design sizes for other fabrics are Aida 11—10⅞″ × 10⅞″; Aida 14—8⅝″ × 8½″; Aida 18—6⅝″ × 6⅝″; Hardanger 22—5½″ × 5⅜″.

MATERIALS for one guest towel
Completed cross-stitch on white Dublin Linen 25 and matching thread—see model information on page 78; 1⅛ yards of ⅜″-wide light green lace trim and matching thread.

DIRECTIONS Cut the Linen 19″ × 26″ with the design centered 3″ from one 19″ edge. Fold ¼″ double to the wrong side of the towel on all edges; stitch the hem. Cut the lace trim in half. Place one length ⅜″ from the finished edge at the design end of the towel; slipstitch. Stitch the second length to the towel ⅛″ from the first length.

MATERIALS for window ornament
Completed cross-stitch on white Dublin Linen 25—see model information on page 78; one 14″ × 14″ piece of lavender fabric; ½ yard of ⅜″-wide light green lace trim; 1 yard of ⅛″-wide white satin ribbon; one 5″-wide Styrofoam ball; glue; small knife.

DIRECTIONS Score a 4½″ circle on the ball using the dull edge of the knife. Center the design piece over the circle and tuck it into the score line, again using the knife. Trim the fabric close to the score line. Center the lavender fabric over the back of the ball and tuck it into the score line. Trim the fabric ¼″ from the score line.

Place the ribbon in the score line and glue in place, leaving loose ends of equal length at the bottom. Tie the ends in a bow. Glue the lace trim to the lavender fabric around the ball ½″ from the score line.

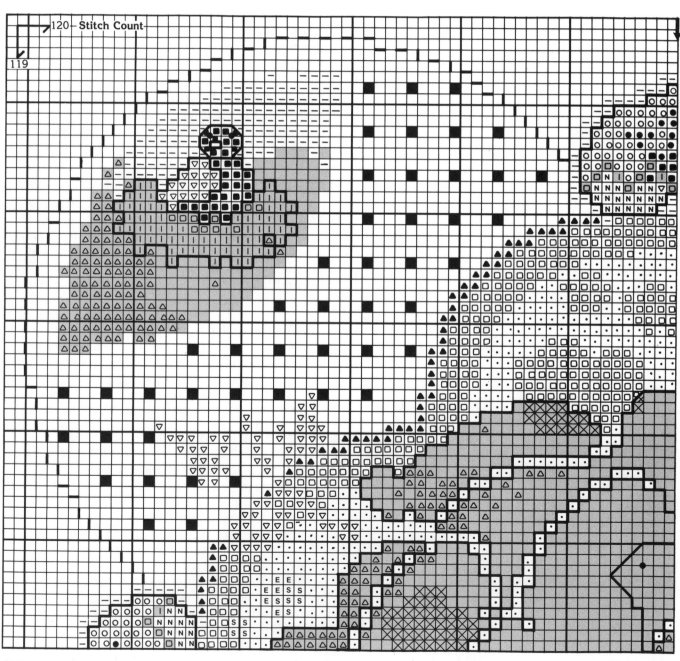

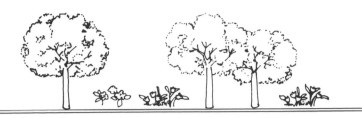

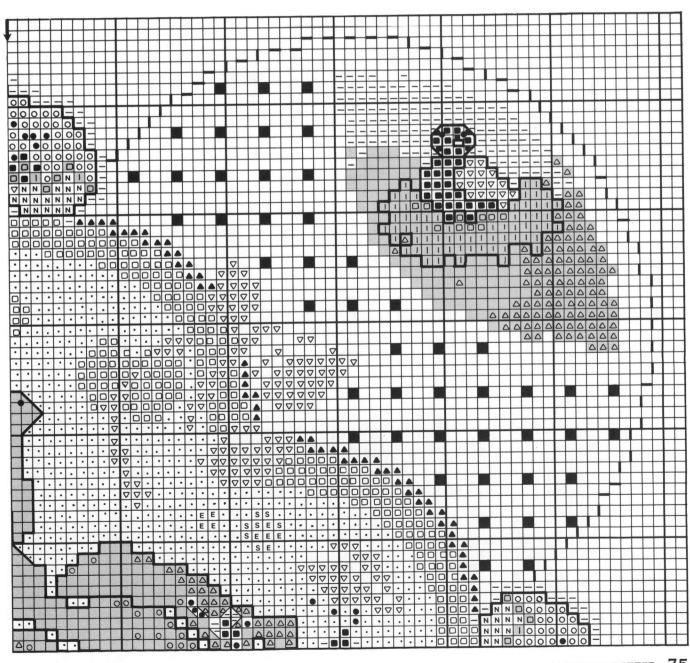

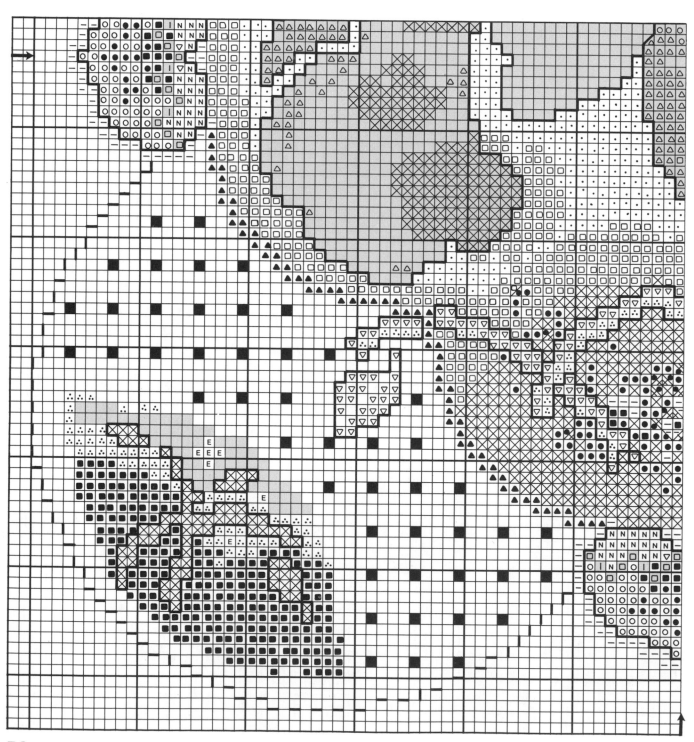

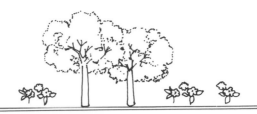

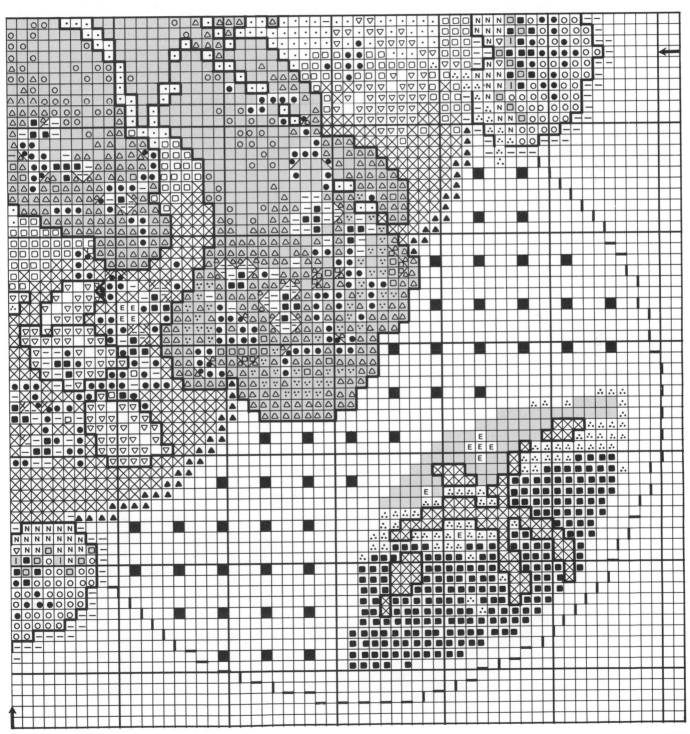

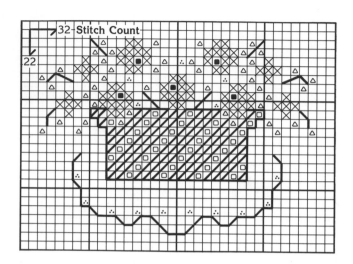

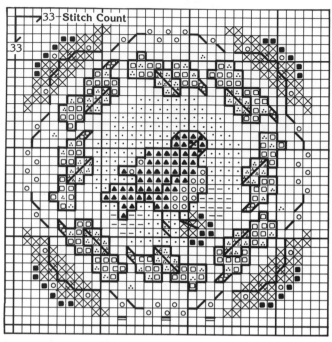

Guest Towels Color Key

Bates		DMC (used for model)	
Step 1:		Cross-stitch (two strands)	
49	▢	3689	Mauve-lt.
117	✕	341	Blue Violet-lt.
121	■	793	Cornflower Blue-med.
214	∴	966	Baby Green-med.
187	△	992	Aquamarine

Bates		DMC (used for model)	
Step 2:		Backstitch (one strand)	
49	⌐	3689	Mauve-lt. (in basket)
121	⌐	793	Cornflower Blue-med. (basket, vine)
187	⌐	992	Aquamarine (stems)

Bates		DMC (used for model)	
Step 1:		Cross-stitch (two strands)	
49	−	3689	Mauve-lt.
105	✕	209	Lavender-dk.
101	■	327	Antique Violet-dk.
117	○	341	Blue Violet-lt.
121	▲ ◣	793	Cornflower Blue-med.
214	· ◿	966	Baby Green-med.
167	▢ ◹	598	Turquoise-lt.
187	∴	992	Aquamarine

Bates		DMC (used for model)	
Step 2:		Backstitch (one strand)	
117	⌐	341	Blue Violet-lt. (outer border)
147	⌐	312	Navy Blue-lt. (bird, leaves)

Step 3:		Beadwork	
	−		Blue hanging bead

MODELS for guest towels Stitch on white Dublin Linen 25 over two threads. The finished design size for one motif is 2½″ × 1¾″. Cut the fabric 21″ × 28″. Center one motif 4¼″ from one end of the towel. Repeat the motif either side of the first motif with four stitches between motifs. Finished design sizes for one motif stitched on other fabrics are Aida 11—3″ × 2″; Aida 14—2¼″ × 1⅝″; Aida 18—1¾″ × 1¼″; Hardanger 22—1½″ × 1″.

MODEL for window ornament Stitch on white Dublin Linen 25 over two threads. The finished design size is 2⅝″ × 2⅝″. Cut the fabric 7″ × 7″. Finished design sizes for other fabrics are Aida 11—3″ × 3″; Aida 14—2⅜″ × 2⅜″; Aida 18—1⅞″ × 1⅞″; Hardanger 22—1½″ × 1½″.

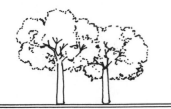

LOVE IS MY GIFT . . .

Even tomboys like to know
that someone loves them.

Bates		DMC (used for model)
Step 1:		Cross-stitch (two strands)
885		739 Tan-ultra vy. lt.
969		316 Antique Mauve-med.
894		223 Shell Pink-med.
871		3041 Antique Violet-med.
871		3041 Antique Violet-med. (ribbon sewn over cross-stitch)
920		932 Antique Blue-lt.
779		926 Slate Green-dk.
875		503 Blue Green-med.
878		501 Blue Green-dk.
Step 2:		Backstitch (one strand)
879		500 Blue Green-vy. dk.
Step 3:		Beadwork
		Old Rose (MPR 553T)
		Mercury (MPR 283)
		Violet (MPR 206T)
		Garnet (MPR 367)
		Emerald (MPR 332)
Step 4:		Ribbonwork (see photo)
		Gray ⅛"–wide silk ribbon with bow (sewn over cross-stitch)
		Green ⅛"–wide silk ribbon bow with streamers

MODEL Stitch on ash rose Lugana 25 over two threads. The finished design size is 9⅝" × 7¾". The fabric was cut 16" × 14". Finished design sizes for other fabrics are Aida 11—11" × 8⅞"; Aida 14—8⅝" × 6⅞"; Aida 18—6¾" × 5⅜"; Hardanger 22—5½" × 4⅜".

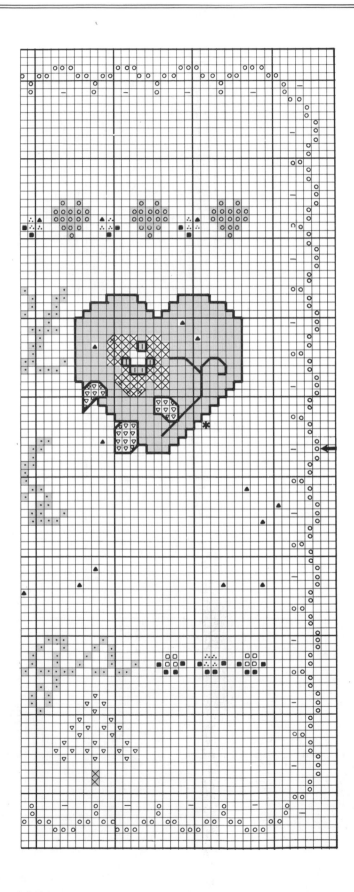

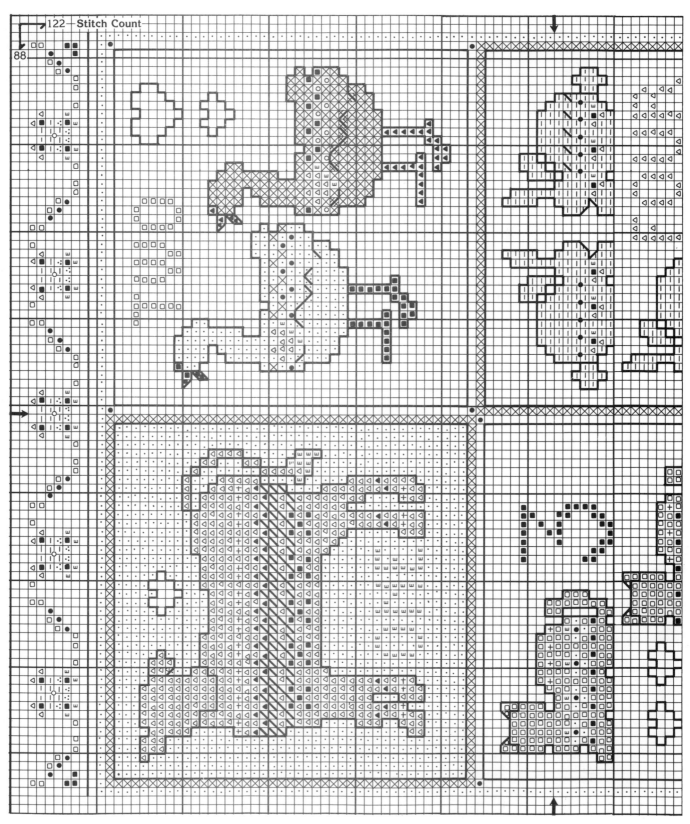

122—Stitch Count

88

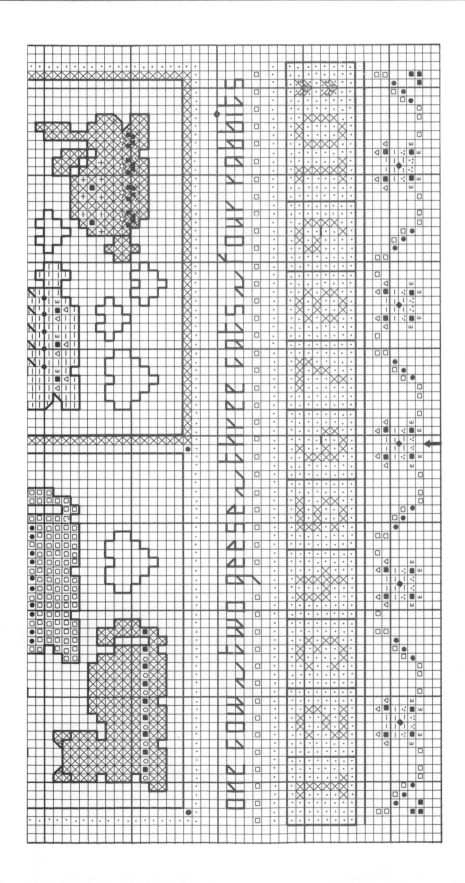

Shhh! Baby's sleeping
and the magic of the moment
is the dream
of a lifetime.

Bates			DMC (used for model)
Step 1:			Cross-stitch (two strands)
1	·	⁄	White
297	▲	⁄	743 Yellow-med.
8	▫	⁄	353 Peach Flesh
323	●		722 Orange Spice-lt.
49	–	⁄	963 Dusty Rose-vy. lt.
74	∴		3354 Dusty Rose-lt.
104	+		210 Lavender-med.
158	o		747 Sky Blue-vy. lt.
167	✕	⁄	598 Turquoise-lt.
168	■	⁄	807 Peacock Blue
882	▵	⁄	407 Sportsman Flesh-dk.
936	ᴇ	⁄	632 Negro Flesh
Step 2:			Backstitch (one strand)
104			210 Lavender-med. (in rabbits)
167			598 Turquoise-lt. (numbers)
168			807 Peacock Blue (hearts, top and bottom border lines, around numbers, in blue duck)
882			407 Sportsman Flesh-dk. (in cow)
936			632 Negro Flesh (all else)
Step 3:			French Knots (one strand)
74	●		3354 Dusty Rose-lt.
168	o		807 Peacock Blue
936	◆		632 Negro Flesh

MODEL for sampler Stitch on yellow Aida 14. The finished design size is 6¼″ × 8¾″. Cut the fabric 13″ × 15″. Finished design sizes for other fabrics are Aida 11—8″ × 11⅛″; Aida 18—4⅞″ × 6¾″; Hardanger 22—4″ × 5½″.

MODELS for soft blocks Stitch the cow square on pink Aida 14, omitting the white background. Stitch the rabbit square on yellow Aida 14. The finished design size is 3⅛″ × 3⅛″. Cut the fabric 6″ × 6″ for each square. Finished design sizes for other fabrics are Aida 11—4″ × 4″; Aida 18—2⅜″ × 2⅜″; Hardanger 22—2″ × 2″.

MODELS for undershirts Stitch the designs, taken from the rabbit square on the graph, on purchased white undershirts using Waste Canvas 14. The finished design sizes are 1¼″ × ⅞″ for the blue rabbit and 2⅝″ × ⅞″ for the pink rabbit pair. Cut the waste canvas 4″ × 2″. Finished design sizes for blue rabbit stitched on other fabrics are Aida 11—1½″ × 1⅛″; Aida 14—1¼″ × ⅞″; Aida 18—1″ × ¾″; Hardanger 22—¾″ × ⅝″. Finished design sizes for pink rabbit pair stitched on other fabrics are Aida 11—3¼″ × 1⅛″; Aida 14—2⅝″ × ⅞″; Aida 18—2″ × ¾″; Hardanger 22—1⅝″ × ⅝″.

MODEL for receiving blanket The design, taken from the cow square on the graph, may be stitched on a purchased white receiving blanket using Waste Canvas 14. The finished design size is 2⅝″ × 2⅜″. Cut the waste canvas 5″ × 5″. Position the design diagonally in one corner 1½″ from the edges of the blanket. Finished design sizes for other fabrics are Aida 11—3¼″ × 3″; Aida 14—2⅝″ × 2⅜″; Aida 18—2″ × 1⅞″; Hardanger 22—1⅝″ × 1½″. Instructions for the crocheted edge are available from Chapelle Designers. Send a self-addressed, stamped envelope to Chapelle Designers, Box 9252 Newgate Station, Ogden, Utah 84409.

MATERIALS for one soft block Completed cross-stitch on pink or yellow Aida 14—see model information; ¼ yard of 45″–wide yellow or blue fabric and matching thread; cream embroidery floss; one 2″–thick foam pillow form for cutting up; quilt batting; white glue.

DIRECTIONS Cut the Aida 4½″ × 4½″ with the design centered. From the yellow or blue fabric, cut five 4½″ × 4½″ pieces. From the pillow form, cut two 4″ × 4″ × 2″ pieces. (An electric knife works nicely.) Glue the foam pieces together to make a cube. Cut the quilt batting into 4½″–wide strips. Wrap the strips around the foam cube once in each direction; glue in place.

Place the Aida piece and one fabric piece with right sides together. Stitch one edge with a ¼″ seam. Add two more fabric pieces to make a strip of four pieces. With the right sides together, stitch the end fabric piece to the Aida to make one continuous piece for the side panel.

With right sides together, place one remaining fabric piece on top of the side panel, matching the corners to the side seams. Stitch with a ¼″ seam, beginning in one corner and stitching to, but not through, the next side seam; backstitch. Repeat to secure remaining three edges. Stitch the remaining fabric piece to the bottom edge of the Aida with a ¼″ seam; do not stitch the remaining three edges.

Insert the foam block. Fold the fabric piece over the block. Turn under ¼″ seam allowance and slipstitch closed. Feather-stitch the Aida seams using one strand of floss.

Made by hand — the way things used to be — means made with the heart.

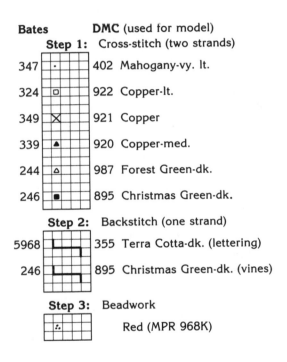

Bates		DMC (used for model)
Step 1:		Cross-stitch (two strands)
347	·	402 Mahogany-vy. lt.
324	▫	922 Copper-lt.
349	✕	921 Copper
339	▲	920 Copper-med.
244	△	987 Forest Green-dk.
246	■	895 Christmas Green-dk.
Step 2:		Backstitch (one strand)
5968		355 Terra Cotta-dk. (lettering)
246		895 Christmas Green-dk. (vines)
Step 3:		Beadwork
	∴	Red (MPR 968K)

MODEL Stitch on cream Belfast Linen 32 over two threads. The finished design size is 4⅜″ × 6¾″. Cut the fabric 11″ × 13″. Finished design sizes for other fabrics are Aida 11—6⅜″ × 9¾″; Aida 14—5″ × 7⅝″; Aida 18—3⅞″ × 6″; Hardanger 22—3⅛″ × 4⅞″.

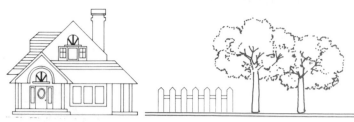

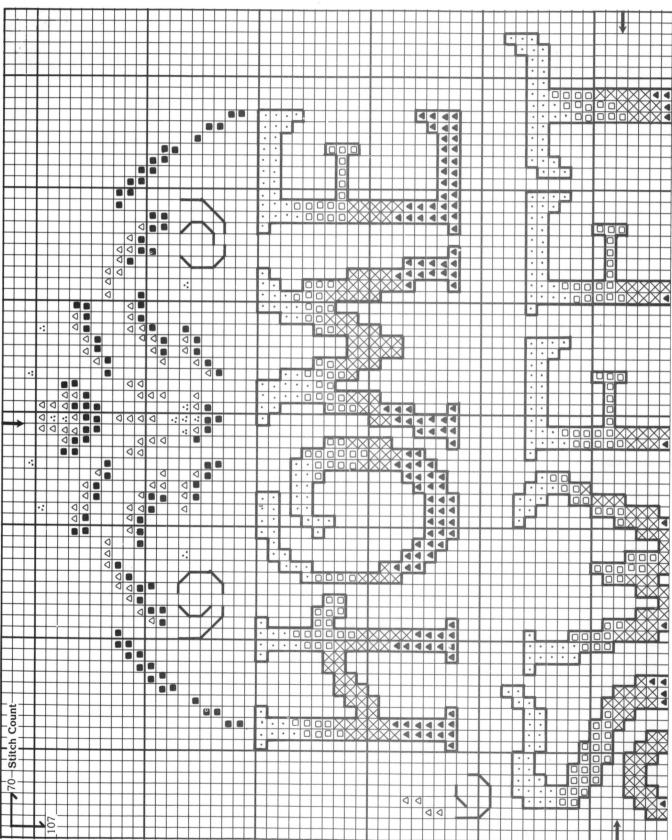

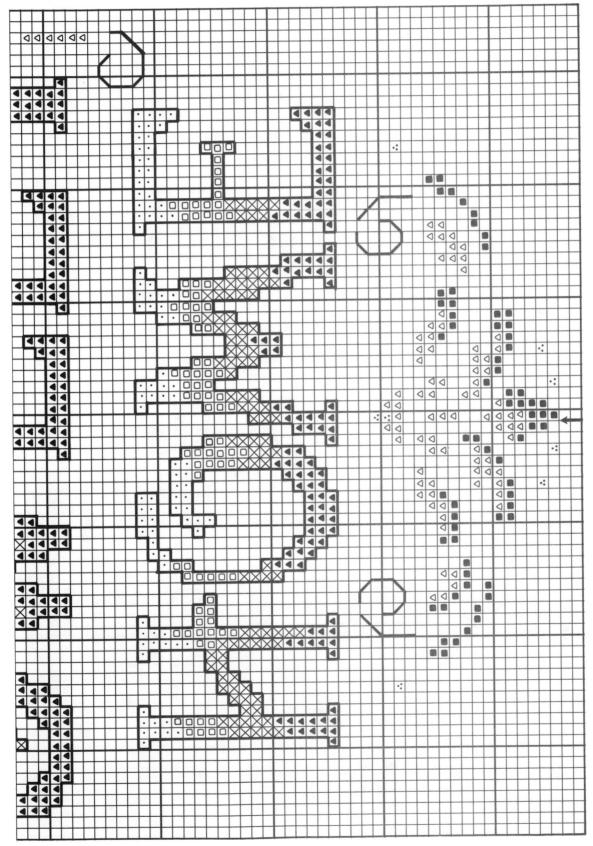

Who is ever caught up on those "nothing" chores? Certainly
no one who loves summer evenings or Saturday mornings.
Certainly no one who reads books or rides bicycles...
Certainly no one...

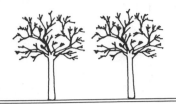

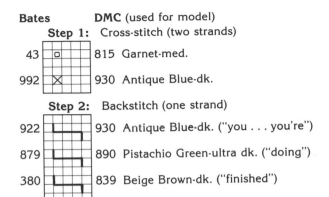

Bates		DMC (used for model)
Step 1:		Cross-stitch (two strands)
43	▫	815 Garnet-med.
992	✕	930 Antique Blue-dk.
Step 2:		Backstitch (one strand)
922		930 Antique Blue-dk. ("you . . . you're")
879		890 Pistachio Green-ultra dk. ("doing")
380		839 Beige Brown-dk. ("finished")

MODEL Stitch on cream Aida 14. The finished design size is 12¼" × 5½". Cut the fabric 19" × 12". Finished design sizes for other fabrics are Aida 11—15½" × 6⅞"; Aida 18—9½" × 4¼"; Hardanger 22—7¾" × 3½".

What was Paradise? but a garden...

— William Lawson

Bates		DMC (used for model)
Step 1:		Cross-stitch (two strands)
297	·	743 Yellow-med.
304	+	741 Tangerine-med.
316	△	740 Tangerine
333	○	608 Orange Red
46	✕	321 Christmas Red
44	■	816 Garnet
27	ı	893 Carnation-lt.
35	∴	891 Carnation-dk.

95	·	554 Violet-lt.
99	●	552 Violet-dk.
168	⊙	518 Wedgewood-lt.
162	+	517 Wedgewood-med.
131	–	798 Delft-dk.
133	▲	796 Royal Blue-dk.
255	▱ ◿	907 Parrot Green-lt.
258	▽	905 Parrot Green-dk.
307	◿	977 Golden Brown-lt.
308	✕ ◿	976 Golden Brown-med.
355	▣ ◿	975 Golden Brown-dk.

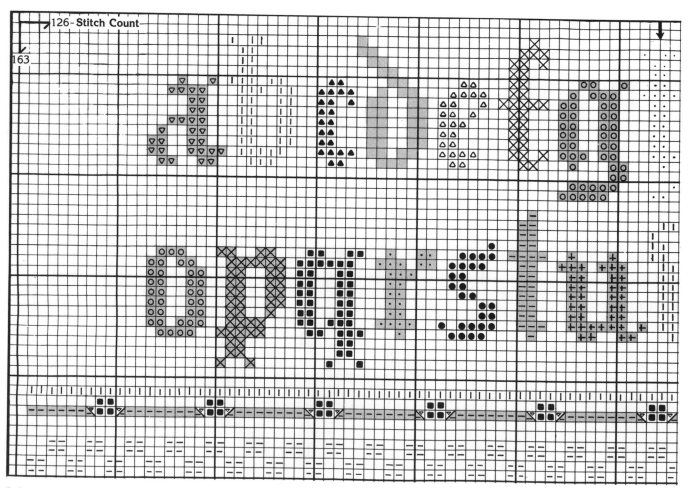

126 – Stitch Count

163

Step 2: Backstitch (one strand)

44		816 Garnet
27		893 Carnation-lt.
99		552 Violet-dk.
133		796 Royal Blue-dk.
258		905 Parrot Green-dk.
355		975 Golden Brown-dk.

Step 3: French Knots

44	●	816 Garnet
27	▲	893 Carnation-lt.
99	■	552 Violet-dk.
133	◇	796 Royal Blue-dk.
355	△	975 Golden Brown-dk.

MODEL Stitch on white Linda 27 over two threads. The finished design size is 9⅜" × 12⅛". Cut the fabric 16" × 19". Finished design sizes for other fabrics are Aida 11—11½" × 14⅞"; Aida 14—9" × 11⅝"; Aida 18—7" × 9"; Hardanger 22—5¾" × 7⅜".

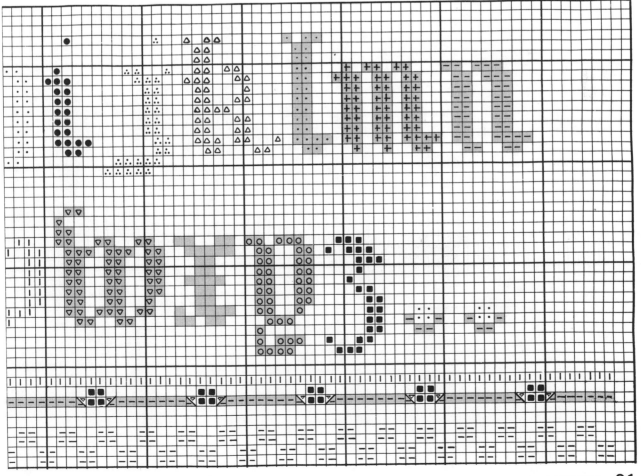

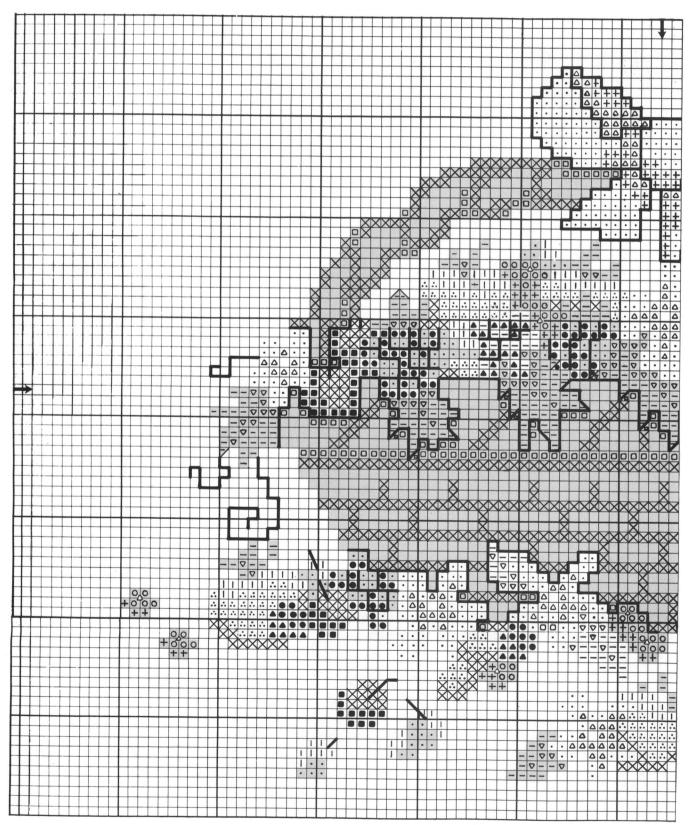

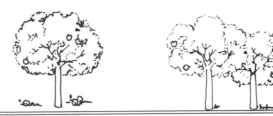

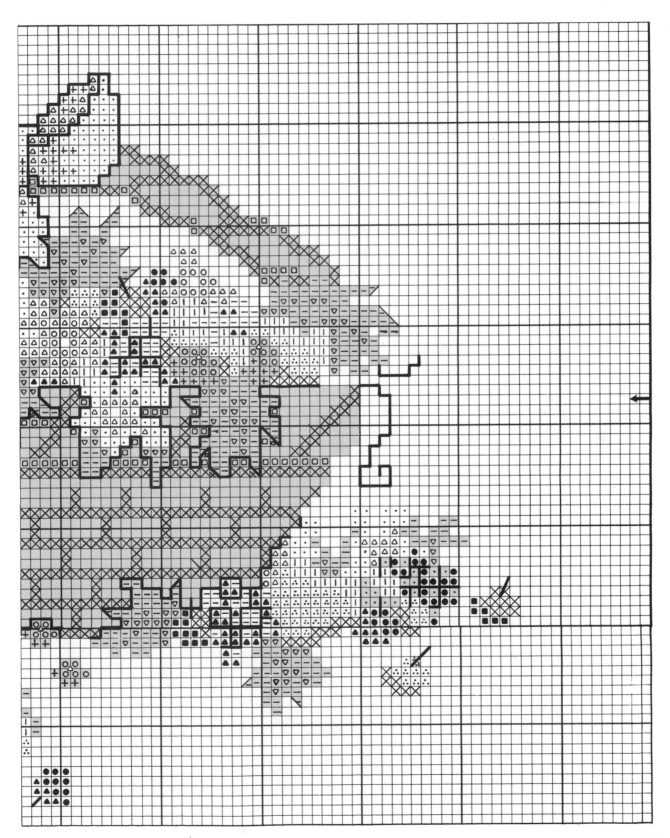

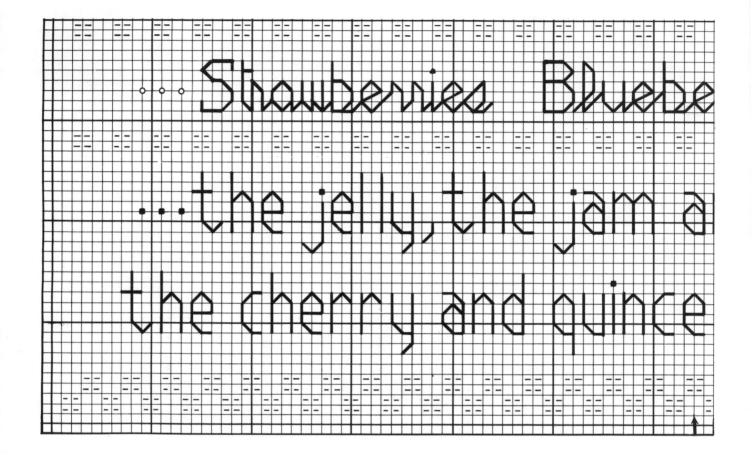

Strawberries Blueber

....the jelly, the jam a

the cherry and quince

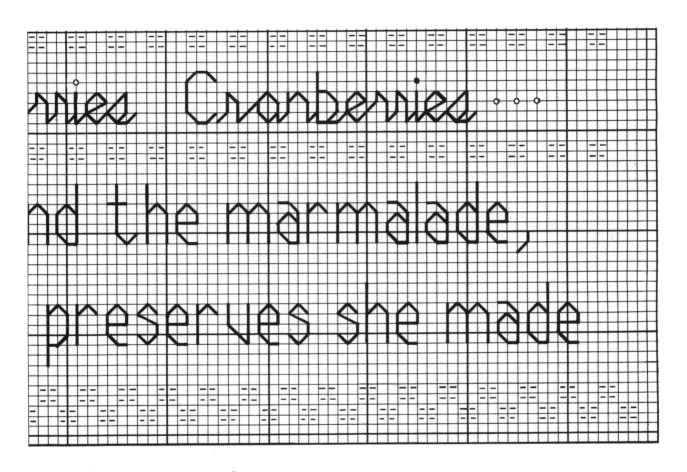

...rries Cranberries... and the marmalade, preserves she made

Step 2: Backstitch (one strand)

44	816 Garnet
27	893 Carnation-lt.
99	552 Violet-dk.
133	796 Royal Blue-dk.
258	905 Parrot Green-dk.
355	975 Golden Brown-dk.

Step 3: French Knots

44	816 Garnet
27	893 Carnation-lt.
99	552 Violet-dk.
133	796 Royal Blue-dk.
355	975 Golden Brown-dk.

1 Find the center of the fabric. Zigzag the edges.

2 Cut the floss into 18″ lengths. Dampen and separate the strands. Put together the strands needed.

3 Locate the center of the design on the graph by following the vertical and horizontal arrows. Begin stitching at the center of the fabric. To make a waste knot, knot the floss and begin on the fabric front 1″ from the design area. Work several stitches over the thread to secure. Cut off the knot.

4 Make one cross for each symbol on the chart. For rows, stitch from left to right, then back. All stitches should lie in the same direction.

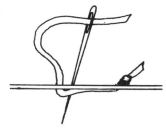

5 For half-crosses, make the longer stitch in the direction of the slanted line on the graph.

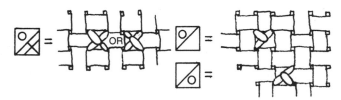

6 Backstitching is used to outline and accent. Use one strand less than for cross-stitch.

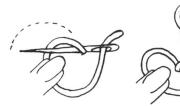

French Knot

Feather Stitch

SOURCES

Cross-stitch products are available retail from Shepherd's Bush, 220 24th Street, Ogden, UT 84401.

Fabrics are available to shop owners from Joan Toggitt, 246 Fifth Avenue, New York, NY 10001.

Beads are available to shop owners from MPR Associates, P.O. Box 7343, High Point, NC 27264 (except blue hanging beads on A Summer Breeze window ornament).

Ribbon is available to shop owners from C. M. Offray & Son, Route 24, Box 601, Chester, NJ 07930-0601.

For use with "Pieces of Time," page 10.

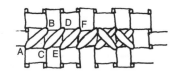